Reading STREET

Grade 3.1

Scott Foresman
Practice Book

PEARSON
Scott Foresman

Editorial Offices: Glenview, Illinois • Parsippany, New Jersey • New York, New York
Sales Offices: Needham, Massachusetts • Duluth, Georgia • Glenview, Illinois
Coppell, Texas • Sacramento, California • Mesa, Arizona

ISBN: 0-328-14519-X

Contents

Unit 3
People and Nature

	Family Times	Comprehension Skills	Lesson Vocabulary	Comprehension Review	Phonics	Research and Study Skills
The Gardener	101–102	103, 107, 108	104, 105	106	109	110
Pushing Up the Sky	111–112	113, 117, 118	114, 115	116	119	120
Night Letters	121–122	123, 127, 128	124, 125	126	129	130
Symphony of Whales	131–132	133, 137, 138	134, 135	136	139	140
Volcanoes	141–142	143, 147, 148	144, 145	146	149	150

Family Times

Summary

Boom Town

The discovery of gold in California brought new settlers with dreams of striking it rich. Some prospectors brought their families and everything they owned. The new settlers needed food, clothes, banks, and schools. In one short year, a town would rise where there had been only a field of wildflowers.

Activity

Build a Boom Town Imagine that your family just sold all of its possessions and hopped on a stagecoach going to California. Together, talk about what you will need when you get there and where you might find those things.

Comprehension Skill

Realism and Fantasy

Realistic stories tell about something that could happen. A **fantasy** is a story about something that could never happen.

Activity

What Happened Today? Ask family members to tell you about things that happened to them today. Ask them to tell things that really did happen and some things that could never happen. Guess which happened and which did not and explain how you could tell.

Lesson Vocabulary

Words to Know

Knowing the meanings of these words is important to reading *Boom Town*. Practice using these words to learn their meanings.

Vocabulary Words

boom a time of fast growth

business the work one does to make money

coins pieces of metal used as money

fetched to have gone after and brought back something

laundry place where clothes are washed and ironed

mending fixing; repairing

pick a pointed tool used to break rocks and loosen dirt

skillet a shallow pan with a handle, used for frying

spell a period of time

Grammar

Sentences

A **complete sentence** tells a complete idea, begins with a capital letter, and ends with an end mark.

Sentence: The dogs run across the grass. They bark happily.

Not a Sentence:

chewing on a bone
playing on the grass

Activity

Making Sentences Players take turns offering a sentence or a part of a sentence. The other players say "sentence" if the sentence is complete. If the phrase is not a sentence, they offer ways to make it a complete sentence.

Not a Sentence	Sentence
are beautiful	Flowers are beautiful.
ten blue balloons	Ten blue balloons rise.
jumping up and down	Crazy kangaroos are jumping up and down.

Practice Tested Spelling Words

_____ _____ _____ _____

_____ _____ _____ _____

_____ _____ _____ _____

_____ _____ _____ _____

_____ _____ _____ _____

Realism and Fantasy • Prior Knowledge

- A **realistic story** tells about something that could happen.
- A **fantasy** is a story about something that could never happen.
- Use your **prior knowledge** and connect what you read with what you already know to help your understanding. You can also use **prior knowledge** to judge whether a story is **realistic** or a **fantasy**.

Directions Read the following passage.

Marcus is a cowboy and Sam is his special horse. Marcus put the saddle on Sam, and then he got on to ride away.

As they left the corral, Sam spread his wings and flew over the fence. They landed in a meadow far away.

"That was fun," said Marcus. "Now let's fly across the Rocky Mountains."

"Okay," said Sam, and he flew over the mountains to the Pacific Ocean. Then he flew back home again.

"You're the best horse I've ever had," Marcus said to Sam.

Directions Complete the chart. Tell what happens and whether it could happen or not. Then tell if the story is a realistic story or a fantasy. Explain why.

What Happens?	Could This Happen? (Check one)	
Sam flies over the fence.	☐ Yes	☐ No
	☐ Yes	☐ No
This story is a		

Home Activity Your child identified a story as a fantasy by finding things that happen in the story that could not happen in real life. Discuss familiar books with your child and ask your child to tell whether the story is a realistic story or a fantasy.

Vocabulary

Directions Choose the word from the box that best matches each definition. Write the word on the line.

_____ **1.** went after or got

_____ **2.** fast-growing

_____ **3.** repairing

_____ **4.** a period of time

_____ **5.** a frying pan

Directions Choose the word from the box that best matches each clue. Write the word on the line.

_____ **6.** This is a tool used for breaking up rocks.

_____ **7.** People use these metal pieces to pay for things.

_____ **8.** This is where you might find stacks of dirty clothes.

_____ **9.** A gas station and grocery store are examples of this.

_____ **10.** Sewing skills are needed for this task.

> ### Check the Words You Know
> ___boom
> ___business
> ___coins
> ___fetched
> ___laundry
> ___mending
> ___pick
> ___skillet
> ___spell

Write a Movie Script

On a separate sheet of paper, tell what would happen in a movie you might make about life in a fast-growing town long ago. Identify the main characters and describe key events in the beginning, middle, and end of the story. Use as many vocabulary words as possible.

© Pearson Education 3

Home Activity Your child identified and used vocabulary words from *Boom Town*. With your child, read a story or nonfiction book about the California Gold Rush. Discuss what it might have been like to live during that period of time. Encourage your child to use vocabulary words in your conversation.

Vocabulary • Context Clues

- **Homonyms** are words that are pronounced and spelled the same but have different meanings.
- Use the words and sentences around the **homonym** to help you figure out what it means.

Directions Read the following passage about life during the Gold Rush. Then answer the questions below. Look for context clues as you read.

Our family decided to head West after we heard about the discovery of gold. As the boat carried us away, we waved to our friends standing on the bank of the river watching us leave. Once we reached the West, it didn't take long to see that we weren't going to strike it rich as miners. For a short spell, we didn't know how we would live. Then Dad had an idea.

He decided the boom town that had grown so quickly near the mines needed a store. The store would sell tools and other supplies that miners needed. The first day we opened, Dad sold a pick and a shovel. After that, business just kept growing.

1. What does *leave* mean in this passage? What clues help you to determine the meaning?

_____

2. What are two meanings for *bank?* What clues tell you the word's meaning here?

_____

_____

3. What does *spell* mean in this passage?

_____

4. What does *boom* mean in this passage? What clues help you know this?

_____

5. In this passage, is a *pick* something you use or something you do? What clues help you to figure this out?

_____

Home Activity Your child used context clues to understand homonyms—words that are pronounced and spelled the same but have different origins and meanings. Provide sentences with homonyms such as *ball* (a round object/a formal dance) or *bat* (a flying animal/a club). Ask your child to use context clues to determine the meaning of each homonym.

© Pearson Education 3

Character

Directions Read the following passage. Then answer the questions below.

Mona's parents own a laundry business. Mona's mother also does mending. Mona always stops in after school. She likes the smell of soap and the noise of coins going into the laundry machine slots.

"Hello, dear," says Mom when Mona enters the laundry. "How was school today?"

"Fine," says Mona. She watches as Mom stitches the hem in a pair of pants.

"I need more blue thread," Mom says to Mona. "Would you mind fetching some for me?"

Mona goes over to her mother's sewing box. She picks out more blue thread and takes it to her mother. Then she hears a noise at the back door.

"That must be your father returning from his errands," says Mom, as Dad pops into the room.

"Howdy!" Dad says, setting down boxes of laundry soap. Mona looks at his cheerful expression and feels happy.

1. Who are the characters in the story?

_____

2. What word in the story tells you what Mona's father is like?

_____

3. How do you know that Mona likes going to the laundry? _____

_____

4. What does Mona do that tells you she is helpful?

_____

5. Write a description of Mona's mother. Tell what she is like and how you know.

_____

_____

_____

_____

© Pearson Education 3

Home Activity Your child identified character traits for several characters in a realistic story. Read a story together that has several characters. Tell who are the characters in the story. Discuss the character traits, or qualities, of each of the characters.

Realism and Fantasy • Prior Knowledge

- A **realistic story** tells about something that could happen.
- A **fantasy** is a story about something that could never happen.
- Use your **prior knowledge** and connect what you read with what you already know to help your understanding. You can also use **prior knowledge** to judge whether a story is **realistic** or a **fantasy**.

Directions Read the following passage. Then answer the questions below.

James and Ted want to go to baseball camp, but they don't have enough money.

"Why don't we sell lemonade?" James said to Ted. "We could put a stand at the corner."

So the two brothers mixed up some lemonade in a pitcher. Then they made a sign that said: LEMONADE 25¢

The boys sold 5 pitchers of lemonade and made $10.

"Let's keep selling until we have enough for camp," said Ted.

1. Could two brothers sell lemonade and make money? _____

2. Is it possible for two boys to make lemonade? _____

3. Do you think the boys could have made $10 in real life? _____

4. Is this story a realistic story or a fantasy? Explain.

_____

_____

_____

5. What did you already know that helped you decide whether the story is realistic or not?

_____

_____

School + Home **Home Activity** Your child was asked questions to decide whether a story was a realistic story or a fantasy. Ask similar questions when you read stories together. Have your child explain his or her answer using prior knowledge.

Realism and Fantasy

- A **realistic story** tells about something that could happen.
- A **fantasy** is a story about something that could never happen.

Directions Read the following passage.

When the Kellys came across the sea to America, Dad got a job sweeping streets. Everyone else got a job at the mill.

Mom wove cloth at a loom. Patrick swept floors. Missy was a bobbin girl. She put new spools of thread on the machines when they were empty.

Mom made a dollar a day. The children made only a few pennies.

"I wish you didn't have to work," said Dad. "But we need the money."

"We'll never get rich," said Patrick.

"Maybe someday we'll start our own business," said Mom. "Then we'll make more money."

Directions Complete the chart. Tell what happens and whether or not it could happen. Then tell if the story is a realistic story or a fantasy. Explain why.

What Happens?	Could This Happen? (Check one)	
Dad gets a job sweeping streets.	☐ Yes	☐ No
	☐ Yes	☐ No
This story is a		

Home Activity Your child identified a story as a realistic story by determining that events in cotton mills one hundred years ago could have happened. Tell your child about events that happened a long time ago. Also, make up some things that could not happen. Ask your child to tell whether the events could really happen or not.

© Pearson Education 3

Short Vowels

Directions Choose the word with the **short vowel** sound in the **first syllable** to complete each sentence. Write the word on the line.

_____ **1.** My mom works in a big (hotel/hospital).

_____ **2.** She got the job last (April/winter).

_____ **3.** She works for a (doctor/painter).

_____ **4.** Mom writes (poems/messages).

_____ **5.** She uses a (pencil/notepad).

Directions Circle the word with the **short vowel** sound in the **first syllable**. Then underline the letter that stands for that short vowel sound.

6. happen	higher	hoses
7. miner	problem	music
8. paper	private	puppet
9. lately	lettuce	likely
10. trial	toaster	tunnel
11. napkin	native	notebook
12. spoken	spider	signal
13. baby	basket	biker
14. sister	safety	season
15. tasteful	timer	tennis

Home Activity Your child identified words with a short vowel sound in the first syllable, such as *happen, lettuce,* and *tennis.* Have your child make a collage of magazine pictures showing items that have a short vowel sound in the first syllable of each item's name. Help your child label each picture.

Advertisement/Poster

An **advertisement** is an announcement that tries to persuade readers, listeners, or viewers to do or buy something or to feel a particular way about something. An advertisement sometimes appears on a **poster** or sign.

Directions Use the poster advertisement to answer the questions that follow.

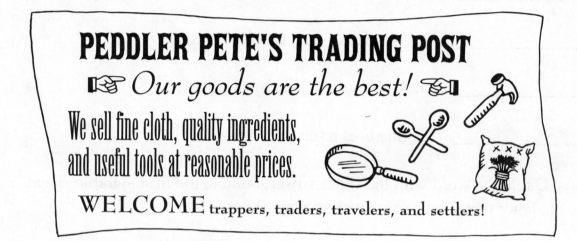

PEDDLER PETE'S TRADING POST
☞ *Our goods are the best!* ☜
We sell fine cloth, quality ingredients, and useful tools at reasonable prices.
WELCOME trappers, traders, travelers, and settlers!

1. What does the advertisement/poster want readers to do?

_____

2. What is one reason for buying goods from this trading post?

_____

3. What kind of people might shop at the trading post?

_____

4. What words are used to help persuade readers?

_____

5. What slogan, or saying, does the advertisement use to describe items sold in the store?

_____

Home Activity Your child used a poster advertisement to answer questions. Have your child create a poster to "sell" one of his or her favorite toys. Encourage your child to use persuasive words and ideas on the poster.

10 Research and Study Skills

Practice Book Unit 1

Family Times

Summary

What About Me?

Once there was a boy who hungered for knowledge. So he went to see a Grand Master who might teach him. But the Grand Master sent him on a hunt for a carpet, which led to a search for thread, and then to a search for goat hair, goats, a goat pen, and a wife for the carpenter. As the boy worked to help others get what they needed, he learned that the best gifts come when a person is giving and that knowledge can come when we least expect it.

Activity

What Can I Do For You? Together, spend an hour doing something for someone else. You might make a neighbor cookies, fix a broken toy for your brother or sister, or leave fun notes for those you love. How did doing something for someone else make you feel? What gift did you get from giving?

Comprehension Skill

Sequence

Sequence is the order in which things happen in a story—what happens first, next, and last. Picturing the story in your mind as you read may help you remember the order of events.

Activity

Teach Me How Think about one of your skills. Are you a good helper in preparing dinner? Can you change your own bicycle tire? Take turns explaining the steps needed to do the task correctly in the order in which they must occur.

Lesson Vocabulary

Words to Know

Knowing the meanings of these words is important to reading *What About Me?* Practice using these words.

Vocabulary Words

carpenter a person who builds and repairs houses and other things made of wood

carpetmaker a person who makes carpets

knowledge an understanding that is gained through experience or study

marketplace a place where food and other products are bought and sold

merchant a person whose business is buying goods and selling them for a profit

plenty more than enough of something

straying wandering or lost

thread very thin cord used in sewing and in weaving cloth

Grammar

Subjects and Predicates

A sentence tells a complete idea with a subject and predicate. A **subject** tells who or what the sentence is about. A **predicate** tells what the subject is or does. In the following sentences, the subject is underlined and the predicate is circled.

The boys climb the tree.

They laugh and play.

Activity

Put It All Together This activity works well on a quick trip in the car or even in line at the supermarket. The first player says a noun and a verb. The other players take turns coming up with the best complete sentence using those two words.

Noun	Verb
cats	nap

Ten silky cats nap in the afternoon sun.

Practice Tested Spelling Words

_____ _____ _____ _____

_____ _____ _____ _____

_____ _____ _____ _____

_____ _____ _____ _____

_____ _____ _____ _____

Sequence • Summarize

- **Sequence** is the order in which things happen in a story—what happens first, next, and last.
- Sometimes a writer uses **clue words** such as *first, so, then,* and *at last.*
- Good readers **sum up** as they read and remember important events in the order they happened.

Directions Read the following passage.

First, Cisco raked leaves for Mrs. Rey. He put the leaves into four piles on the lawn.

Cisco could not put the leaves in plastic bags by himself. So Cisco asked his brother Rico to help.

Rico held the bags open, and then Cicso dumped leaves inside. When a bag was full, Cicso tied it at the top.

At last they were done, and Mrs. Rey gave Cisco twenty dollars. Cisco gave Rico five dollars for helping.

Directions Write these sentences in the correct place on the organizer.

- Cisco put leaves in a bag.
- Cisco asked Rico to help.
- Mrs. Rey paid Cisco $20.
- Cisco raked the leaves.

1. First

↓

2. Next

↓

3. Then

↓

4. Last

5. On another piece of paper, use the sentences to write a summary of the story.

Home Activity Your child put events from a story in the order they happened. Read a simple story to your child. Name events from the story by asking, "What are some things that happened in the story?" Then ask your child to retell the story putting the events in the order they happened.

Vocabulary

Directions Write the word from the box that best completes each sentence.

> ## Check the Words You Know
>
> ___carpenter   ___merchant
> ___carpetmaker   ___plenty
> ___knowledge   ___straying
> ___marketplace   ___thread

_____ 1. Sara had _____ of clothes to mend.

_____ 2. She needed to buy _____ for sewing.

_____ 3. She walked to the _____ to go shopping.

_____ 4. She found a _____ who sold what she wanted.

_____ 5. Later she talked to the _____ about a new rug.

Directions Write the word from the box that best matches each clue.

_____ 6. a person who builds with wood

_____ 7. a lot

_____ 8. wandering or roaming

_____ 9. facts and ideas

_____ 10. someone who makes rugs

Write an Interview

On a separate paper, write five questions you could ask a carpenter, merchant, or a carpetmaker. Answer each question. Use as many vocabulary words as possible.

Home Activity Your child identified and used vocabulary words from *What About Me?* With your child, act out a conversation that might have taken place in an old-time village marketplace. Use vocabulary words as you and your child discuss what you are buying or selling.

© Pearson Education 3

Vocabulary • Word Structure

- Sometimes you may come across a word you don't know. The word may be a long **compound word** made up of two small words.
- If you know the meaning of the small words, it will help you figure out the meaning of the long compound word.

Directions Read the riddle. Then circle the compound word that solves the riddle.

1. I take care of goats. I watch them during the day. I watch them at night. Who am I?

   goatkeeper   goaltender

2. I sit and weave all day. I make wonderful patterns of many colors. I make things you put on your floor and walk on. Who am I?

   coverup   carpetmaker

3. I raise goats. When they are big, I sell them to people. Who am I?

   cowboy   goatseller

4. I help people get married. I help a man meet a woman that he will like. I help a woman meet a man she will like. Who am I?

   matchmaker   firefighter

5. I am a place where people go to buy things. There are many people selling things here. There are many people buying things here. What am I?

   doorknob   marketplace

6. I am a place for children. I have swings and monkey bars. I have many things that children can play on. What am I?

   playground   outline

7. Birds live inside me. I have a perch for them to sit on. I have cups for food and water. What am I?

   cardboard   birdcage

8. I own a store. I help my customers. I stand behind the counter. People who buy things in my shop pay me. Who am I?

   shopkeeper   airport

Home Activity Your child used word structure to figure out the meaning of unfamiliar compound words. Read a newspaper article or store advertisement with your child. Encourage your child to identify unfamiliar compound words by defining the small words that make up each compound word.

Author's Purpose

Directions Read the following passage. Then answer the questions below.

A carpenter made a beautiful table. He asked his mule to help him take the table to the marketplace.

The carpenter tied the table to the mule's back, and they started down the path. Soon the mule was tired. The mule saw some shade under a large tree, but he kept going.

Then the mule saw a stream of fresh water. The mule wanted to take a drink, but he kept going.

Finally, they arrived at the town. The carpenter sold the table to a merchant. Then he put the mule in the shade and gave the mule plenty of water and food to eat.

Moral: Working hard leads to a reward.

1. What did the mule get as a reward for his hard work?

_____

_____

2. The mule wants to stop twice on the trip to town, but he doesn't. Why do you think the author tells us this?

_____

_____

3. Why do you think the author writes mainly about the mule?

_____

_____

4. What does the reader learn about the most in this story—travel, hard work, or how to behave? Explain.

_____

_____

5. Why did the author most likely write this selection?

_____

_____

Home Activity This story is a fable, or a short story that teaches a lesson. Your child answered questions about the author's purpose, or the reason an author writes a story. After reading a story with your child, stop to discuss why the author wrote the story. Some reasons are to persuade, to entertain, to inform, or to express feelings.

© Pearson Education 3

Sequence • Summarize

- **Sequence** is the order in which things happen in a story—what happens first, next, and last.
- Sometimes a writer uses **clue words** such as *first, so,* and *then*.
- Good readers **sum up** as they read and remember important events in the order they happened.

Directions Read the following passage. Then answer the questions below.

George wanted a blue kite. He didn't have a kite of his own, but he had lots of marbles and a plan. First, he would ask Tammy if she would trade stickers for some marbles. Tammy said, "Okay, I do want some marbles, but why do you want stickers?"

"You'll see," said George.

Then, George took the stickers to Sam. He asked Sam to trade his blue kite for the stickers. Sam was excited to see his favorite stickers, so he traded with George. "That was my plan," said George. "Now we all have something we wanted!"

Finally, George unwrapped the blue kite. He held on tight to the string. The kite flew into the sky. George was happy.

1. Who had the marbles first?

_____

2. Who got the marbles next?

_____

3. What did Tammy give to George?

_____

4. The last event to happen in the story is George flying the kite. What clue word lets you know that?

_____

5. Write a summary of the story.

_____

_____

_____

Home Activity Your child answered questions about the order in which events happened in a story. As you read other books together, write some of the events on cards. Then ask your child to put the cards in the correct order.

© Pearson Education 3

Sequence

- **Sequence** is the order in which things happen in a story—what happens first, next, and last.
- Sometimes a writer uses **clue words** such as *first, so, then,* and *after.*

Directions Read the following passage.

A shepherd named Kit sat by the sea as his sheep ate grass nearby.

I should sell the sheep and become a merchant, thought Kit. And so he did.

Then Kit bought some apples. He put the apples on a wagon to take them to market.

It began to storm. The wind blew strong. The wagon fell over and all of the apples were ruined.

After that, Kit wished he would have kept his sheep.

Directions Write these sentences in the correct place on the organizer.

- The wagon fell over.
- Kit bought some apples.

- Kit sold his sheep.
- Kit sat by the sea.

1. First

↓

2. Next

↓

3. Then

↓

4. Last

© Pearson Education 3

Home Activity Your child put events from a story in the order they happened. Read a simple story to your child. Write four events from the story on cards. Ask your child to arrange the cards in the order the events happened in the story.

Plurals

Directions Use the plural form of each word in ( ) to complete each sentence. Write the word on the line.

_____ 1. Tanya put her hands into her (pocket).

_____ 2. She pulled out a handful of (penny).

_____ 3. She also found two (pencil).

_____ 4. She traded each pencil for two boxes of (paint).

_____ 5. She used the money to buy two new (brush).

_____ 6. She filled (glass) with water for cleaning her brushes.

_____ 7. She painted a forest filled with trees and (bush).

_____ 8. She made pictures of (beach) and waves.

_____ 9. She showed (family) having fun together.

_____ 10. Tanya gave away many (copy) of her pictures.

Directions Write the plural form of each word below.

11. lady _____   **16.** supply _____

12. dish _____   **17.** fox _____

13. class _____   **18.** boss _____

14. peach _____   **19.** list _____

15. kiss _____   **20.** book _____

© Pearson Education 3

School + Home

Home Activity Your child wrote plurals—words naming more than one person, place, or thing. Ask your child to look around a room in your home and tell what he or she sees. Work with your child to write a list of twenty things in the room. Ask your child to write the plural form of each word.

Alphabetical Order

Entries or subjects in encyclopedias, dictionaries, and indexes are listed in **alphabetical order,** so you can find information quickly and easily. When two entries or subjects have the same first letter, alphabetize by the second letter. If the second letters are also the same, alphabetize by the third letter, and so on. See how these occupation entries have been alphabetized in an index.

Accountant, 12	Butcher, 35	Counselor, 14
Actor, 22	Carpenter, 18	Dancer, 23
Auto mechanic, 32	Carpet Installer, 20	Dentist, 29
Bank Teller, 34	Cashier, 9	Designer, 24
Barber, 8	Chef, 7	Educator, 26
Bus Driver, 10	Computer Operator, 6	Engineer, 19

Directions Put these words from *What About Me?* in alphabetical order. Use the index example above to help you.

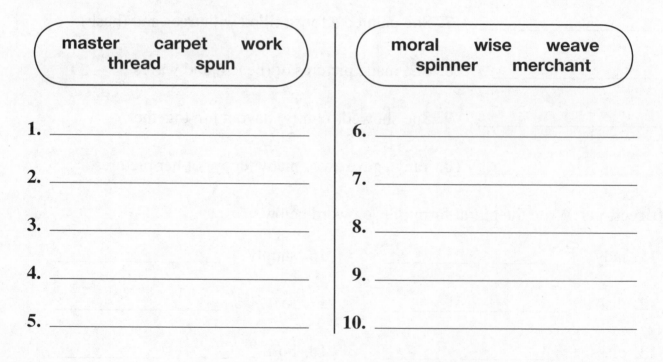

master   carpet   work
thread   spun

moral   wise   weave
spinner   merchant

1. _____

2. _____

3. _____

4. _____

5. _____

6. _____

7. _____

8. _____

9. _____

10. _____

© Pearson Education 3

Home Activity Your child put words in alphabetical order. Give your child a list of 5 names of family members and/or friends. Ask him or her to put the names in alphabetical order.

Family Times

Summary

Alexander, Who Used to Be Rich Last Sunday

Alexander is the youngest of three brothers who each receive a dollar from their visiting grandparents. He means to save the dollar to buy a walkie-talkie, but over the course of the day he spends some of it, loses some of it, and must use some of it to pay for bad decisions. At the end of the day, his dollar is gone, so he sits and thinks about where the money went and how he feels about it all.

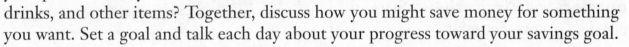

Activity

High Finance This week, keep track of how much money you spend. What do you spend each day on bus fare, hot lunch, drinks, and other items? Together, discuss how you might save money for something you want. Set a goal and talk each day about your progress toward your savings goal.

Comprehension Skill

Sequence

Sequence is the order in which things happen in a story. Sometimes a writer uses clue words like *first*, *then*, *next*, and *finally*.

Activity

All Mixed Up Take turns telling stories about the events of your day, but mix up the order of events. Then have the listener try to figure out the correct order of events using prior knowledge and clues in your story.

Lesson Vocabulary

Words to Know

Knowing the meanings of these words is important to reading *Alexander, Who Used to Be Rich Last Sunday*. Practice using these words.

Vocabulary Words

college a school that offers higher education than high school

dimes coins in the United States equal to ten cents

downtown the main part or business part of a town

fined punished by making someone pay money for breaking a rule

nickels coins in the United States equal to five cents

rich having much money, land, or other valuable things

quarters coins in the United States equal to twenty-five cents

Grammar

Statements and Questions

A **statement** tells something. It begins with a capital letter and ends with a period. A **question** asks something. It begins with a capital letter and ends with a question mark.

Statement: Today is sunny.

Question: What is the weather today?

Activity

Ask and Tell Players take turns thinking of a question. Each partner responds with two statements that answer the question. Players then switch roles.

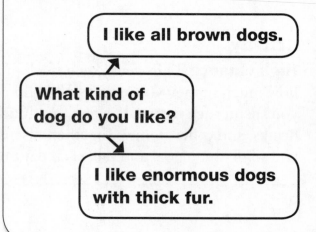

I like all brown dogs.

What kind of dog do you like?

I like enormous dogs with thick fur.

Practice Tested Spelling Words

_____ _____ _____ _____

_____ _____ _____ _____

_____ _____ _____ _____

_____ _____ _____ _____

Sequence • Visualize

- **Sequence** is the order in which events happen in a story. Look for these **clue words:** *first, after, finally.*

- As you read, **visualize** the characters and what is happening to help keep track of the sequence of events.

Directions Read the following passage.

First, Frankie put five dollars in the bank. Dad said they would do this every month.

After four months, Frankie thought, "I have twenty dollars in the bank!"

After eight months, Frankie thought, "I have forty dollars in the bank!"

Finally, Frankie had saved for one year. He got a letter from the bank. It said that Frankie had sixty-five dollars in the bank.

"But I saved only sixty dollars," said Frankie.

"You made five dollars this year," said Dad. "The bank pays you for keeping money in the bank."

Directions Write the important events in the correct place on the time line. Then answer the question.

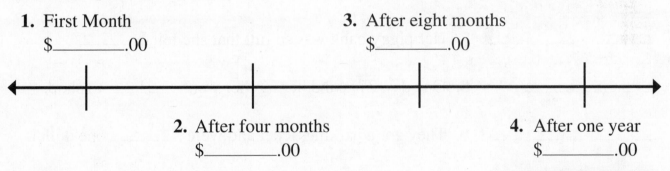

1. First Month
   $_____.00

3. After eight months
   $_____.00

2. After four months
   $_____.00

4. After one year
   $_____.00

5. Picture Frankie in your mind when his dad tells him that he made five dollars. Describe what Frankie looks like.

_____

_____

Home Activity Your child ordered events in a story. Name four events that happened in your family during the last year. Do not tell them in the order they happened. Ask your child to put them in the correct order. Encourage your child to use the words *first, then, next,* and *finally.*

Vocabulary

Check the Words You Know

___college   ___nickels
___dimes   ___quarters
___downtown   ___rich
___fined

Directions Draw a line to match each word with its definition.

1. rich   coins worth ten cents each

2. nickels   having much money

3. fined   center of town

4. dimes   ordered to pay money for breaking a law

5. downtown   coins worth five cents each

Directions Write the word from the box that best completes each sentence.

_____ 6. Tina saved most of her money to pay for _____ .

_____ 7. Her piggy bank was so full that she felt _____ .

_____ 8. One day, Tina and her mother went _____ to shop.

_____ 9. They got a parking ticket and were _____ one dollar.

_____ 10. Tina gave her mother four _____ to pay the fine.

Write an Essay

On a separate sheet of paper, write an essay explaining why it is important to save. Use as many vocabulary words as possible.

Home Activity Your child identified and used vocabulary words from *Alexander, Who Used to Be Rich Last Sunday*. Ask your child to help you count loose coins, such as nickels, dimes, and quarters. Talk about their value, what you or your child could do with them and why it is important to save money. Use as many vocabulary words as possible.

© Pearson Education 3

Vocabulary • Glossary or Dictionary

- Sometimes you come across a word you don't know. You can use a **glossary** or a **dictionary** to find the meaning of the unfamiliar word.

- A **glossary** has the meanings of important words in a book. A **dictionary** has the meanings of many words. Both have words in alphabetical order.

---

college *n.* a school one attends after high school
dime *n.* a coin worth ten cents
downtown *n.* a part of a city or town with stores and offices

fined *v.* money paid as punishment for doing something wrong
quarter *n.* a coin worth 25 cents, or one-quarter of a dollar
rich *adj.* having a lot of money

Directions Each sentence has one underlined word. Use the dictionary entries above to find the meaning. Write the meaning of the word on the line.

1. I gave the man four <u>quarters</u>, and he gave me one dollar.

_____

2. My dad <u>fined</u> me one dollar for not doing my chores.

_____

3. The <u>rich</u> man had a large house with a swimming pool.

_____

4. When Grandma was little, it cost two nickels to ride the bus <u>downtown</u>.

_____

5. My babysitter goes to <u>college</u> to study teaching.

_____

6. On holidays my Aunt Dee comes for dinner and always gives me ten <u>dimes</u>.

_____

 Home Activity Your child used sample dictionary entries to learn the meaning of unfamiliar words. Read a story or magazine article about money together and look up unfamiliar words. Encourage your child to look up unfamiliar words in the dictionary while reading.

© Pearson Education 3

Draw Conclusions

- A **conclusion** is a decision you reach after you think about details and facts.
- As you read, think about the details and facts and **what you already know** to **draw conclusions** about characters and the things that happen.

Directions Read the following passage. Then answer the questions below.

> Peter works at a store after school. On Monday, Mrs. Wick asks Peter to stack cans of beans. She gives Peter five nickels. When Peter goes home, he puts the nickels in his nickel jar.
>
> On Wednesday, Mrs. Wick asks Peter to sweep the floor. She gives Peter three dimes. When Peter goes home, he puts the dimes in his dime jar.
>
> On Friday, Mrs. Wick asks Peter to take a sack of food to the lady next door. She gives Peter a quarter. When Peter goes home, he puts the quarter in his quarter jar.
>
> That weekend, Peter looks at his jars of money. *I'm not rich*, he thinks, *but someday I will use this money to go to college.*

1. How do you know that Peter is a hard worker?

_____

2. Which days does Peter probably work each week?

_____

3. Why do you think Peter has a job?

_____

4. How much money did Peter earn this week?

_____

_____

5. How do you think Peter feels as he looks at the money in his jars?

_____

_____

Home Activity To answer the above questions, your child practiced the skill of drawing conclusions. The author does not always tell everything in a story. Sometimes, readers have to draw conclusions to understand what happened. Read a realistic fiction story with your child. Ask your child questions that require drawing conclusions.

Sequence • Visualize

- **Sequence** is the order in which events happen in a story. Look for these **clue words:** *first, then, next,* and *last.*

- As you read, **visualize** the characters and what is happening to help keep track of the sequence of events.

Directions Read the following passage. Then answer the questions below.

Tina's mother liked to look at rainbows. Tina decided to make her mom a rainbow. First she found some red and orange buttons which she glued onto a piece of paper.

Then Tina used the glue and added some yellow and green glitter under the red and orange buttons.

Next she glued some old scraps of blue and indigo colored fabric under the yellow and green glitter.

Last she used some violet colored paint to finish her work of art. Now her mom can see a beautiful rainbow at any time.

1. When did Tina find the red and orange buttons?

_____

2. What did Tina glue on the paper after the red and orange buttons?

_____

3. When did Tina use the scraps of blue and indigo colored fabric?

_____

4. What color did Tina use last?

_____

5. Picture the sequence that Tina followed. Why did she do things in this order?

_____

_____

© Pearson Education 3

Home Activity Your child answered questions about the order that events happened in a story. Write the events from this story on cards or pieces of paper. Ask your child to put the cards in the correct order.

Sequence

- **Sequence** is the order in which events happen in a story. Look for these **clue words**: *first, next, then,* and *last.*
- As you read, **visualize** the characters and what is happening to help keep track of the sequence of events.

Directions Read the following passage.

First, Ben took the money out of his piggy bank. He had three dollars and twenty-five cents. *Not enough money,* he thought.

Then, Inez raked leaves. She got one dollar. *We need more money,* she thought.

Next, Alex found three quarters in the sofa. *Now we have enough money,* he thought.

Finally, the children went to the store. They got a vase for their mother's birthday. The vase cost five dollars.

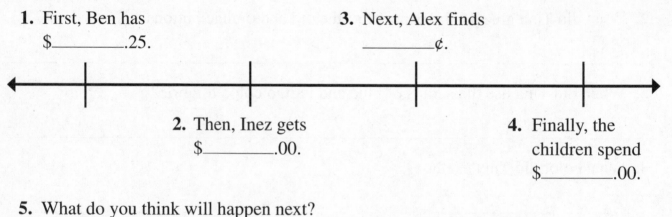

Directions Write the money amounts from the story in the correct place on the time line. Then answer the question.

1. First, Ben has
   $_____.25.

3. Next, Alex finds
   _____¢.

2. Then, Inez gets
   $_____.00.

4. Finally, the
   children spend
   $_____.00.

5. What do you think will happen next?

_____

_____

© Pearson Education 3

Base Words and Endings

Directions Add **-ed** and **-ing** to each word on the left. Remember that you may have to double the last consonant, drop the final **e**, or change **y** to **i**.

Word	-ed	-ing
plan	**planned**	**planning**
1. please	_____	_____
2. use	_____	_____
3. shop	_____	_____
4. worry	_____	_____
5. tug	_____	_____

Directions Add **-er** and **-est** to each word on the left. Remember that you may have to double the last consonant, drop the final **e**, or change **y** to **i**.

Word	-er	-est
heavy	**heavier**	**heaviest**
6. great	_____	_____
7. easy	_____	_____
8. thin	_____	_____
9. angry	_____	_____
10. big	_____	_____

Home Activity Your child wrote words that ended with *-ed, -ing, -er,* and *-est*. Work with your child to write a story using the words on the page above. Before the writing begins, ask your child to review the words he or she wrote and think about ways to use the words.

Skim and Scan

Readers **skim** to find the main idea of a text. Skimming is reading quickly and not reading every word. To skim, read titles, headings, and some sentences. Readers **scan** to look for certain words or phrases. Scanning can be used to find out if a text or resource has the information a reader wants or if it answers a question.

Directions Skim or scan the chart to answer each question.

Making and Using Money

How to Earn It	How to Save It	How to Spend Wisely
• Do yard work for neighbors • Do odd jobs • Return bottles and cans for cash	• Put it away where you won't see it all the time • Put it in the bank	• Make a list of things you want • Spend money only on things on the list

1. What kind of information is in the first column?

_____

2. What is one way to earn money?

_____

3. Who might skim the information in this table?

_____

4. What is one way to save money?

_____

5. Which column would you read to find ways to buy what you want?

_____

Home Activity Your child has learned to skim and scan text. Have your child skim and scan a newspaper or magazine article to determine the main idea.

Family Times

Summary

If You Made a Million

In this story by David M. Schwartz, a friendly magician shows you the relative size of different amounts of money. Looking at gradually larger amounts of money, the magician takes you from a simple penny to a million dollars. Along the way, he explains interest in a savings account, the use of checks, and the way a bank loan works. At the end, the magician sums up his lessons by reminding the reader that "Making money means making choices."

Activity

Is It Worth It? As you run errands together, such as purchasing groceries or buying gas, look at the total amount of the purchase. How much is that worth? For example, thirty dollars worth of gas might buy 25 loaves of bread or one video game. Which is the best use of your money? What circumstances might affect your answer?

Comprehension Skill

Realism and Fantasy

Realistic stories tell about something that could happen. A **fantasy** is a story about something that could never happen.

Activity

What Could You Buy? Describe things you would want to buy if you had a million dollars, such as a flying carpet or enough ice cream to fill up your kitchen. Explain whether each thing could really be bought or could never be bought.

Lesson Vocabulary

Words to Know
Knowing the meanings of these words is important to reading *If You Made a Million*. Practice using these words.

Vocabulary Words

amount the sum of two or more numbers or quantities

check a written order directing a bank to pay a certain amount of money to the person named

earned deserved or won because of hard work or good behavior

expensive having a high price; very costly

interest money that is paid for the use of borrowed or deposited money

million 1,000,000

thousand 1,000

value the worth of something in money

worth equal in value to

Grammar

Commands and Exclamations
A **command** tells someone to do something. It begins with a capital letter and ends with a period. An **exclamation** tells something with very strong emotion. It begins with a capital letter and ends with an exclamation point.

Command: Put the cup on the table.

Exclamation: This apple is delicious!

Activity
What Kind? Players take turns thinking of a sentence. Each partner responds by naming the kind of sentence. Players then switch roles.

statement	question	command	exclamation
The sky is blue.	Is it sunny today?	Look out the window.	The sun is so bright!

Practice Tested Spelling Words

_____ _____ _____ _____

_____ _____ _____ _____

_____ _____ _____ _____

_____ _____ _____ _____

Realism and Fantasy • Monitor and Fix Up

- A **realistic story** tells about something that could happen.
- A **fantasy** story could never happen. Some stories are mostly realistic but may include events that are fantasy.
- **Check your understanding** as you read. If you are not sure about something, you can **reread** parts.

Directions Read the following passage.

> Jennifer had a loose tooth. When she was brushing her teeth, she noticed that the tooth had fallen out. She looked into the sink, and the tooth was not there. She checked to see if it was stuck in her toothbrush and then looked into the sink again. The tooth was missing. Jennifer had really lost her tooth! Out of the corner of her eye she saw something moving. Then she heard something cheerfully say, "I found it!" Her toothbrush was pushing the missing tooth toward her.

Directions Complete the chart. Tell what's real and what's not. Then tell if the story is a realistic story or a fantasy.

What's Real?	What's Not?
1. Jennifer had a loose tooth.	4.
2.	5.
3.	

6. This story is a _____ .

Home Activity Your child identified a story as a fantasy by finding something in it that could not happen in real life. List all of the events in the story for your child in the order they happened. Ask if each event could really happen. Explain that if just one thing happens that isn't real, the story is a fantasy.

© Pearson Education 3

Vocabulary

```
┌─────────────────────────────────────────┐
│      Check the Words You Know            │
│                                           │
│   ___amount         ___worth              │
│   ___value          ___earned             │
│   ___interest       ___expensive          │
│   ___check          ___thousand           │
│   ___million                              │
└─────────────────────────────────────────┘
```

Directions Fill in the blank with the word from the box that fits the meaning of the sentence.

1. The actor said the lady doesn't know the _____ of a dollar.

2. That gold ring is _____ a lot of money.

3. Money that you save in a bank earns _____.

4. If I had one dollar more than $999, I'd have one _____ dollars.

5. That skyscraper cost about twenty _____ dollars to build.

Directions Draw a line from the word to its definition.

6. expensive   what something is worth

7. amount   costs a lot of money

8. check   worked for money

9. earned   a written order for a bank to pay money

10. value   the total sum

Write a Story

On a separate sheet of paper, write a story about someone who wins a lot of money. Describe how the money is won and spent. Use as many vocabulary words as possible.

© Pearson Education 3

Home Activity Your child identified and used words from *If You Made a Million Dollars*. Read a story or newspaper article about money. Discuss the story or article with your child using this lesson's vocabulary words.

Vocabulary • Context Clues

- Sometimes you may come across a word you don't know. The word might have two meanings.
- Use **context clues**—the words around the unfamiliar word—to help you figure out its meaning.

Directions Read each sentence. One word is underlined in each sentence. There are two meanings written below each sentence. Circle the meaning of the underlined word.

1. My money earns <u>interest</u> while it's in my account.

   curiosity   money paid by the bank

2. Please <u>check</u> to see if the water is boiling.

   look at carefully   an order written to pay money from a bank

3. My aunt <u>raises</u> horses on her farm.

   lifts   takes care of

4. I am trying to <u>save</u> enough money to buy a bike.

   rescue   set aside

5. We went fishing near the <u>banks</u> of the river.

   places you keep money   land that edges the water

6. My father paid the gas <u>bill</u> by writing a check to the gas company.

   charge   paper money

7. Your money <u>grows</u> if you let it stay in the bank a long time.

   gets taller   increases in amount

8. It's time for me to <u>leave</u> for school.

   let alone   go out

Home Activity Your child used context clues to figure out the meaning of words that have two meanings. Read a story about money with your child. Encourage him or her to identify any words that have two meanings and to use context clues to figure out what they mean.

Sequence of Events

Sequence is the order in which events happen in a story. Look for **clue words** such as *first, then, next,* and *last.*

Directions Read the following passage. Then answer the questions below.

Billions of coins are made at the U.S. Mint. First, round disks are punched out of sheets of metal. The blank rounds are heated until they are soft, and then they are run through a washer and dryer.

Next, all of the blank coins are checked to see if they are the right size and shape. The blanks go through a mill that raises a rim around their edges. Then they are sent through a press that stamps a design and words on each coin.

Different presses make different kinds of coins. Each kind of coin has a different value. The dollar coins are worth the greatest amount.

When the coins are finished, they are checked again for any mistakes. Then a counting machine counts them and drops them by the thousands into bags. A forklift takes the bags to a vault.

1. What must be done first when making coins?

_____

2. What happens just before the coins are run through a washer and dryer?

_____

3. After the blank coins are checked, what happens next?

_____

4. What happens to the coins after they are finished?

_____

5. If you can't remember the order of the steps, what can you do to check your understanding?

_____

Home Activity To answer the above questions, your child used knowledge of sequence, or the order in which things happen. Make up a story about a task you do around the house, such as washing the car or doing the dishes. Use the words *first, next,* and *finally.* Then ask your child questions about what happened first, next, and last.

© Pearson Education 3

Realism and Fantasy • Monitor and Fix Up

- A **realistic story** tells about something that could happen.
- A **fantasy** story could never happen. Some stories are mostly realistic but may include events that are fantasy.
- **Check your understanding** as you read. If you are not sure about something, you can **reread** parts.

Directions Read the following passage. Then answer the questions below.

> Joy had five dollars. It wasn't enough money to buy the new pair of jeans she wanted.
>
> Joy put her five-dollar bill under a chicken in the chicken coop. The next morning, she went out to gather eggs.
>
> Instead of one five-dollar bill, she now had four five-dollar bills!
>
> "The chicken laid five-dollar bills!" Joy said. She went right to the store and bought her pair of jeans.

1. Is it realistic that a child might want a new pair of jeans?

_____

2. Is it possible for a child to put a five-dollar bill under a chicken?

_____

3. Do you think Joy is right when she says the chicken laid five-dollar bills?

_____

4. If the chicken laid the five-dollar bills, what kind of story is it?

_____

5. Check your understanding. What if you read on and find this out:
The extra five-dollar bills were put in the chicken's nest by Joy's father.
Then what kind of story is it?

_____

Home Activity Your child determined whether events in a story could really happen or not. Name these events and decide whether it's possible that a child could do them in real life: play the piano well (yes), talk to a chicken (yes), hold a conversation with an owl (no), stay up all night (yes), run faster than a parent (yes), grow wings and fly (no).

Realism and Fantasy

- A **realistic selection** could really happen. **Nonfiction** writing gives facts and is realistic.
- In a **fantasy**, things happen that are not real. A **fantasy** is fiction writing, but **nonfiction** writing can give facts about a fantasy.

Directions Read the following passage.

Do you like books? You can read lots of books at a library. Most people have favorite stories—ones they like better than others. Which story do you like best? Some like the story of Peter Rabbit.

In this story, a rabbit goes into a garden. The owner chases him. Peter loses a shoe and his jacket. Peter gets away, but he is sick. His mother makes him drink tea. He has to stay in bed.

Directions Complete the chart. Tell what's real and what's not.

What's Real?	What's Not?
1. Reading books at a	3. A rabbit wears
2. A story about	4. The rabbit mother gives Peter

5. Using what you know about rabbits, write two nonfiction sentences telling about how real rabbits live.

_____

_____

_____

Home Activity Your child identified some things in writing that are fantasy. Read stories in which animals talk, wear clothes, and do other things that humans do. Discuss whether animals really do these things. Ask your child whether the stories are real or imaginary.

© Pearson Education 3

Long Vowel Digraphs

Directions Choose the word with the **long a**, **long e**, or **long o** sound that best matches each definition. Write the word on the line.

_____ 1. all right   glad   okay   well

_____ 2. a sound of pain   groan   sob   whimper

_____ 3. free from dirt   clean   fresh   spotless

_____ 4. toss   fling   pitch   throw

_____ 5. go along with   accept   admit   agree

_____ 6. reach or get   gain   gather   win

_____ 7. heat until brown   cook   toast   broil

Directions Circle the word that has the **long a**, **long e**, or **long o** sound. Then underline the letters in the word that stand for that vowel sound.

8. chock	chop	cheep
9. best	blown	bought
10. flash	float	flock
11. braid	brick	build
12. school	sorry	stay
13. feast	flash	friend
14. dish	dream	droop
15. sand	screen	shoe
16. plain	plant	print

Home Activity Your child wrote words in which the long *a* sound is spelled *ay* and *ai*, the long *e* is spelled *ee* and *ea*, and the long *o* is spelled *oa* and *ow*. Ask your child to list words that rhyme with the long *a*, *e*, and *o* words on the page above. Write the rhyming words and have your child read them noting different spellings for the same sound.

Parts of a Book

Books have different parts that help you find the information you need. At the front, a **table of contents** lists chapters, articles, or stories and their page numbers. An **index** lists subjects that the book covers and tells the page on which the information can be found. An index is usually in the back of the book.

Directions Use the table of contents and the index to answer the questions.

Table of Contents **Money Around the World**	**Index**
Chapter 1 North and South America 3	**Dollar** 　Australia, 32 　Canada, 5 　Taiwan, 14 　United States, 4
Chapter 2 Europe and Asia 10	**Euro** 　List of Countries, 10
Chapter 3 Africa and Australia 25	

1. In which chapter will you look if you want to read about money in South America?

_____

2. On which page will you look to find the countries that use the Euro as money?

_____

3. Which chapter has information about the Australian dollar?

_____

4. On which page is there information about the Canadian dollar?

_____

5. Chapter 3 starts on which page?

_____

Home Activity Your child used a table of contents and index to answer questions. Ask your child to locate information using a table of contents and index in a favorite book.

Family Times

Summary

My Rows and Piles of Coins

Saruni helps his mother sell her goods at the market every Saturday. After each day of sales, she gives him a few coins to spend on anything he wants. But Saruni has a dream of helping his mother by buying a bicycle to take her goods to market. He saves his coins each week while he learns to ride a bicycle. He saves for months, and, with the help of his mother and father, finally gets his bike. As soon as he has it, he comes up with a new plan to help her.

Activity

Helping Others Together, talk about the people or groups that matter to you. How could you help them? Could you organize a bake sale, a group yard sale, or provide help with their activities? Set some goals and try to meet them.

Comprehension Skill

Character and Setting

A **character** is a person who takes part in the events of a story. The **setting** is when and where a story takes place.

Activity

Your Favorite Story Think about your favorite story. Tell who the characters are in the story and where it takes place. Talk about some things the characters do and how they feel about these things.

Words to Know

Knowing the meanings of these words is important to reading *My Rows and Piles of Coins*. Practice using these words.

Vocabulary Words

arranged put in order or position

bundles things tied or wrapped together so that they are easier to carry

dangerously unsafely

errands short trips to do something

excitedly with strong lively feelings

steady firmly fixed; not swaying

unwrapped uncovered by removing something placed around an item

wobbled moved from side to side in an unsteady or shaky way

Grammar

Compound Sentences

A **compound sentence** is made up of two simple sentences joined with a comma and a word such as *and* or *but*. To make a compound sentence, write the first sentence. Put a comma in place of the end punctuation and add a word such as *but*. Then add the second sentence, but begin it with a lowercase letter unless it is a proper noun or *I*.

Example: I took my notebook, but I forgot to take my pencil.

Activity
Making Compound Sentences

One player is the writer. All players think of simple sentences. There should be at least two sentences for each topic. The writer records each sentence on a scrap of paper. When there are at least six simple sentences, players lay the paper scraps face up on the table. Players then take turns choosing two sentences that go together and making them into a compound sentence.

Practice Tested Spelling Words

Character and Setting • Story Structure

- A **character** is a person or animal who takes part in the events of a story. You can learn about characters by their words and actions.
- The **setting** is when and where a story takes place.
- Use the **story structure**—beginning, middle, and end—to learn about **characters** and **setting**.

Directions Read the following passage. Then complete the chart below.

Ebu's family owns a salt mine in North Africa. Ebu is only 10 years old. He reads about faraway cities and sees them on TV, but there is no other place he would rather live.

Ebu helps tie salt slabs onto the camels. They journey through the desert.

At night, Ebu helps feed the camels. Then he eats food cooked over a fire.

Ebu and his family arrive at Timbuktu. They set up their stall. Soon all of their salt has been sold.

Characters	Setting
1. Name and age	3. Where story takes place
2. Character trait	4. When story takes place

5. Write the sentence in the last paragraph that describes the setting.

_____

_____

Home Activity Your child answered questions about a story's characters and setting. Name stories your child is familiar with and ask your child to list the characters in it. Then ask where and when the story takes place.

Vocabulary

Check the Words You Know	
___errands	___bundles
___steady	___wobbled
___dangerously	___arranged
___unwrapped	___excitedly

Directions Fill in the blank with the word that fits the meaning of the sentence.

1. Hold the ladder _____ so I can climb up.

2. I _____ often when I first learned to ride a bike.

3. He _____ his birthday presents after the party.

4. She did a few _____ to help her grandmother.

5. We tied our clothes in _____ and went to the laundry.

Directions Draw a line from the word to its definition.

6. dangerously   put in order

7. arranged   shook from side to side

8. excitedly   uncovered

9. unwrapped   in an unsafe way

10. wobbled   with strong, lively feelings

Write an Advertisement

On a separate sheet of paper, write an advertisement for a job. Write about someone who is looking for a student to work after school. Describe the job and how much it pays. Use as many vocabulary words as possible.

© Pearson Education 3

Home Activity Your child identified and used words from *My Rows and Piles of Coins*. Read a story about a student who gets a job. Discuss the story with your child using this lesson's vocabulary words.

Vocabulary • Word Structure

- Sometimes you may come across words you do not know. You can look to see if the base word has a **prefix** at the beginning or a **suffix** at the end that helps you figure out the meaning.

- The **prefix** un- makes a word mean "not" or "the opposite of." For example, unhappy means "not happy."

- The **suffix** -ly makes a word mean "in a ___ way." For example, slowly means "in a slow way."

Directions Read each sentence. One word is underlined in each sentence. Circle the prefix un- or suffix -ly in the underlined word. Then circle the correct meaning of the word.

1. When I <u>unloaded</u> the heavy things from the bike, it was easy to ride.

   took off   put on

2. I was <u>deeply</u> pleased when I won the prize.

   a strongly felt way   very low

3. The boy stood <u>dangerously</u> close to the edge of the cliff.

   in an unsafe way   in an angry way

4. She <u>unwrapped</u> the gift and found ice skates inside.

   took off the cover   did not open

5. He laughed <u>gleefully</u> when he won the spelling bee.

   in a silly way   in a happy way

6. After the hike, we returned <u>wearily</u> to our tents and went to sleep.

   very quickly   in a tired way

7. My father <u>proudly</u> gave me a hug when he saw my report card.

   in a loud way   in a pleased way

8. I <u>untied</u> the bundle of coins and gave my sister a dime.

   opened   spilled

Home Activity Your child used prefixes and suffixes to figure out the meaning of words. With your child, read a story about a person who gets a part-time job to earn money. Encourage your child to find words that have prefixes and suffixes and to use them to figure out the meaning of unfamiliar words.

Realism and Fantasy

A **realistic story** tells things that could happen. A **fantasy** story could never happen.

Directions Read the following passage. Then answer the questions below.

Hong lives in Chinatown. Her parents make fortune cookies. Sometimes Hong runs errands. Sometimes she helps put small papers in the cookies. The papers tell a fortune. The cookies are sold to Chinese restaurants all over the United States.

"Today will be fun," says Hong excitedly. "It's the day of the big parade."

Hong sits on the curb with her friend. Soon they see huge paper dragons coming down the street.

The dragons wobble. They come dangerously close to the curb. Hong can see the steady feet of the people carrying them.

Bundles of firecrackers are set off. Then children start to play games in the street. Soon everyone is laughing and eating dim sum.

Hong unwraps a cookie. The fortune says, "Save money."

1. Do you think Chinatown is a real place? Explain why.

_____

2. Would a story about live dragons be real or make-believe? How do you know?

_____

3. How do you know that the dragons in this story are not real?

_____

_____

4. Are fortune cookies real or make-believe? How do you know?

_____

_____

5. Check the story's beginning, middle, and end.
Does anything happen that could not happen in real life? _____

What kind of story is it? _____

Home Activity Your child determined whether a story is a realistic story or a fantasy. For a story to be a fantasy, it must include at least one thing that cannot happen in real life. Ask your child to retell familiar stories. Then ask if the story is a realistic story or a fantasy. If the story is a realistic story, ask your child to change the story to include something that could not really happen. Then ask what kind of story it is (fantasy).

© Pearson Education 3

Name _____

Character and Setting • Story Structure

- A **character** is a person who takes part in the events of a story. You learn about characters by their words and actions.
- The **setting** is when and where a story takes place.
- Use the **story structure**—beginning, middle, and end—to learn about characters and setting.

Directions Read the following passage. Then answer the questions below.

Fatima was born in Morocco. Now her family lives in New York City. Her father owns a gas station.

Mother wants to visit Morocco. Fatima and her brothers talk to Dad. They set up a car wash at the gas station.

They wash cars all summer. They save every penny they make.

"By fall, we can give the money to Mother," says Fatima. "Then she can go to Morocco."

1. What is the setting of this selection?

_____

2. How do you know Fatima wants her mother to be able to visit Morocco?

_____

3. Why do you think Fatima's mother wants to visit Morocco?

_____

4. What clues tell you that this story takes place in the present time?

_____

5. Reread the story's beginning, middle, and end. What does each part tell you about Fatima?

_____

_____

Home Activity Your child answered questions about a story's characters. We can learn more about characters by what they say and do. Ask this question: Which of the following words describe Fatima? Then list these words and ask your child to respond by saying yes or no: mean (no), helpful (yes), loving (yes), hard-working (yes), problem-solver (yes), greedy (no), flexible (yes).

© Pearson Education 3

Character and Setting

- A **character** is a person or animal who takes part in the events of a story. You learn about characters by their words and actions.
- The **setting** is when and where a story takes place.

Directions Read the following passage.

Kelly's friends ride bicycles on the road past Kelly's farm. Kelly wants to join them, but she doesn't have a bike.

Every day Kelly helps with the farm chores. She gathers eggs. She feeds pigs. She weeds the family garden. On Fridays, Kelly's dad gives her ten dollars.

Kelly saves each ten-dollar bill. Finally, she has eighty dollars. Her dad takes her into town to get a bike.

When Kelly's friends ride by, Kelly hops on her bike. Now, when her chores are done, she can go riding with her friends.

Directions Complete the chart.

Character	Setting
1. Name	**3.** Where story takes place
2. Character trait	**4.** When story takes place

5. Reread the story's beginning, middle, and end. What does each part tell you about Kelly?

_____

_____

_____

© Pearson Education 3

School + Home **Home Activity** Your child answered questions about a story's character and setting. Ask your child to name as many places as he or she can think of. Suggest places your child likes to visit as well as states and countries. Tell your child that these places could be the setting for a story.

Vowel Diphthongs

Directions Circle each word with **ou** or **ow** that has the same vowel sound as **out**. Then write the word on the line.

_____ 1. Jen slowly counted her money.

_____ 2. She had the amount she needed.

_____ 3. Jen was proud that she didn't have to borrow money.

_____ 4. She could buy her mother some bath powder.

_____ 5. Jen would also buy some yellow flowers.

Directions Circle each word with **oi** or **oy** that has the same vowel sound as **toy**. Then write the word on the line.

_____ 6. It was time for Al to make a choice.

_____ 7. Should he find a new employer?

_____ 8. Al wanted to avoid a long ride to work.

_____ 9. He wanted to enjoy his job.

_____ 10. He also hoped to work in an office that was not noisy.

Directions Circle each word with the same vowel sound as the first word. Then underline the letters in the circled word that stand for that vowel sound.

11. **town**	loyal	proud	snow
12. **boy**	sound	know	broil
13. **choice**	coat	plow	spoil
14. **hour**	crown	float	show
15. **join**	bay	annoy	brown

Home Activity Your child wrote words with the vowel sound in *out*, spelled *ou* as in *proud* and *ow* as in *shower* and the vowel sound in *toy*, spelled *oi* as in *choice* and *oy* as in *voyage*. Have your child list other words that have the vowel sounds in *out* and *toy*. Tell your child to underline the letters that stand for the vowel sound in each word.

Graphs

Graphs help you compare information in numbers. **Pictographs** use pictures or symbols. **Circle graphs** are shaped like a pie and show information in sections of the circle.

Directions The pictograph below shows the money Sam earned selling lemonade. The circle graph shows what coins he has in his money box. Use one of the graphs to answer each question. Tell which graph you used.

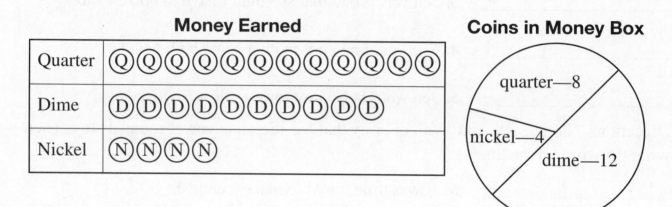

Money Earned

Quarter	Ⓠ Ⓠ Ⓠ Ⓠ Ⓠ Ⓠ Ⓠ Ⓠ Ⓠ Ⓠ Ⓠ Ⓠ
Dime	Ⓓ Ⓓ Ⓓ Ⓓ Ⓓ Ⓓ Ⓓ Ⓓ Ⓓ Ⓓ
Nickel	Ⓝ Ⓝ Ⓝ Ⓝ

Coins in Money Box

quarter—8
nickel—4
dime—12

1. How many dimes did Sam earn selling lemonade?

_____

2. How much are the nickels worth in the money box?

_____

3. How many quarters are in the money box?

_____

4. How many coins are in the money box in all?

_____

5. How many quarters did Sam earn selling lemonade?

_____

Home Activity Your child answered questions by interpreting data in a pictograph and a circle graph. Get a group of different kinds of coins. Have your child count how many there are of each kind and make a pictograph or circle graph to show the results.

Summary

Penguin Chick

A mother and father emperor penguin have only one baby a year. In Antarctica, there is nothing to build a nest with, so the father must keep the egg warm. The mother goes in search of food. The baby hatches shortly before the mother returns. She feeds the baby and cares for him while the father goes to eat and bring back food. The mother and father continue to take turns caring for and feeding the chick until the baby penguin is old enough to go hunt for food on its own.

Activity

Feed the Family Imagine that you have no refrigerator and no garden. You can only eat fresh foods, but the food is many days away! How will you make sure that there is always someone at home to watch the children and always someone collecting food? Discuss your solution.

Comprehension Skill

Main Idea and Supporting Details

The **topic** is what a piece of writing is about. The **main idea** is the most important idea about the topic. **Supporting details** are small pieces of information that tell about the main idea.

Activity

Cook Up a Story Find a very large mixing bowl and place inside of it a slightly smaller bowl. Into this bowl, place many measuring cups. Explain that the biggest bowl is the topic, the smaller bowl is the main idea, and the cups are details. Together, draw the organizer and brainstorm ideas for a story.

Lesson Vocabulary

Words to Know

Knowing the meanings of these words is important to reading *Penguin Chick*. Practice using these words to learn their meanings.

Vocabulary Words

cuddles holds close and tenderly

flippers broad, flat limbs on a penguin used for swimming and moving along on land

frozen hardened with cold; turned into ice

hatch to come from an egg

pecks strikes something with the beak in a quick, short motion

preen to smooth or clean with the beak

snuggles holds closely for warmth, protection, or affection

Grammar

Common and Proper Nouns

A **common noun** names any person, place, or thing. A **proper noun** names a particular person, place, or thing.

Common nouns: girl, city, school

Proper nouns: Lucy, Houston, John Adams Elementary School

Activity

Ten Questions The first player thinks of a proper noun and offers a common noun as a clue. Then the other players ask questions to gather clues about the proper noun. The player who correctly identifies the proper noun chooses the next proper noun.

Practice Tested Spelling Words

_____ _____ _____ _____

_____ _____ _____ _____

_____ _____ _____ _____

_____ _____ _____ _____

_____ _____ _____ _____

Main Idea and Details • Graphic Organizers

- The **topic** is what a piece of writing is about. The **main idea** is the most important idea about the **topic**. **Supporting details** are small pieces of information about the **main idea**.

- A **graphic organizer** can help organize information as you read.

Directions Read the following passage. Complete the graphic organizer below.

What if you wanted to cross Antarctica? What would you need to take along?

You would need warm clothes, such as a parka and fur-lined boots. You'd also need bulky socks, thick pants, and the warmest mittens you could find!

Don't forget to bring your own food. You could warm frozen casseroles over a fire and eat nuts and snack bars during the day.

At night you'll need a sleeping bag. Take the warmest one you can find so you are sure to keep warm all night long!

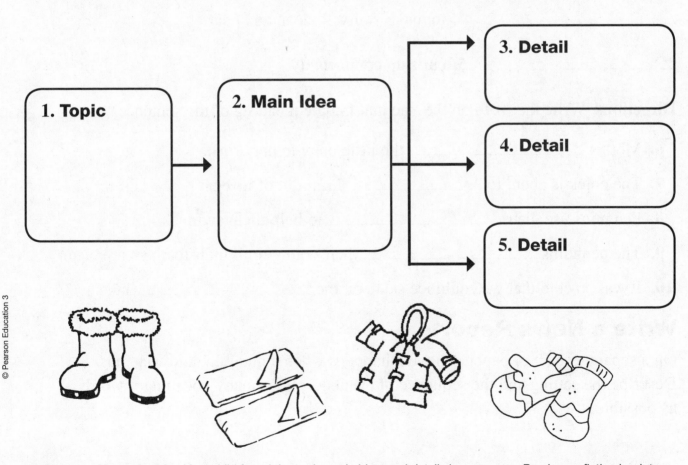

1. Topic

2. Main Idea

3. Detail

4. Detail

5. Detail

© Pearson Education 3

School + Home

Home Activity Your child found the topic, main idea, and details in a passage. Read a nonfiction book to your child. To find the topic, ask, "In one word, what is the book all about?" To find the main idea, help your child make a sentence that tells the most important part about the topic. Then ask your child to list several details that tell more about the main idea.

Vocabulary

Check the Words You Know

___hatch   ___pecks

___snuggles   ___preen

___flippers   ___frozen

___cuddles

Directions Choose the vocabulary word from the box and write it next to its meaning.

_____ **1.** taps at

_____ **2.** turned into solid ice

_____ **3.** limbs used for swimming

_____ **4.** to make yourself clean and neat

_____ **5.** curls up comfortably

Directions Write the word on the line that fits the meaning of the sentence.

6. Mother _____ the little baby in her arms.

7. The chick is about to _____ out of its egg.

8. Penguins use their _____ to help them swim.

9. The penguins _____ their young until their feathers are clean.

10. It was so cold that we could ice skate on the _____ lake.

Write a News Report

On a separate sheet of paper, tell what happens when a penguin chick hatches. Describe the setting and the sequence of events using as many vocabulary words as possible.

School + Home   **Home Activity** Your child identified and used vocabulary words from *Penguin Chick*. Read a story or a nonfiction article about penguins with your child. Discuss the story using this week's vocabulary words.

Vocabulary • Context Clues

- Sometimes you come across a word you don't know. The author may give you a clue about its meaning. The clue may be a **synonym**, a word that means the same thing.
- Look for **synonyms** to figure out the meaning of unfamiliar words.

Directions Read the sentences. One word is underlined. Circle the synonym of the underlined word. Write the meaning of the underlined word on the line.

1. The chick <u>pecks</u> at the inside of the egg. After the chick taps a hole in the egg, the chick can leave the egg.

_____

2. She made an <u>error</u> in her spelling, so she fixed the mistake.

_____

3. Joe can put on his <u>flippers</u> or his fins to swim quickly.

_____

4. Penguins <u>preen</u> their chicks by cleaning and brushing them with their beaks.

_____

5. The penguin chick must <u>stay</u> on its mother's feet to remain warm.

_____

6. Penguins hunt <u>creatures</u> of the sea, such as the tiny animals called krill.

_____

7. The newborn chick was very <u>fluffy</u>, with soft and fuzzy feathers all over it.

_____

8. Like human children who love hugs, penguin chicks love to <u>cuddle</u>.

_____

Home Activity Your child used context clues such as synonyms to figure out the meaning of new words. Read a story together and encourage your child to find synonyms in the text that help to figure out the meaning of unfamiliar words.

© Pearson Education 3

Sequence of Events

Sequence is the order in which events happen in a story. Look for **clue words** such as *first, then, next,* and *last.*

Directions Read the following passage. Then answer the questions below.

Most birds lay their eggs in nests. Robins lay blue eggs in a nest high in a tree. A mother robin usually lays four eggs, one egg each day.

Then the mother snuggles up to the eggs to keep them warm. While she sits there, she may preen her feathers to keep herself clean.

Tiny babies hatch from the eggs in about two weeks. Each baby pecks at the egg until finally it can get out. Then the baby bird cuddles up to the mother to keep warm. The babies also cuddle with each other.

Both parents bring worms for the growing babies to eat. In about two weeks, the babies are ready to fly away. Then they can find food for themselves.

1. What is the first stage in the life of a robin?

_____

2. What does the mother robin do after she lays the eggs?

_____

3. When are the babies ready to hatch?

_____

4. During what stage does the father robin help?

_____

_____

5. How would a chart help you keep track of the life cycle of a robin?

_____

_____

Home Activity Your child learned the sequence, or stages, in the life of a robin. Read a book about a different life cycle, perhaps one about butterflies. When finished, ask your child to tell what stage happens first, next, and last.

© Pearson Education 3

Name _____

Main Idea and Details • Graphic Organizers

- The **topic** is what a piece of writing is about. The **main idea** is the most important idea about the **topic**. **Supporting details** are small pieces of information about the **main idea**.
- A **graphic organizer** can help organize information as you read.

Directions Read the following passage. Then answer the questions below.

Every summer, Jamie's family goes to a beach to swim in the warm waters. Jamie's mom and dad like to snorkel. They breathe through a tube. They wear goggles so they can see the colorful fish. But Jamie does not swim well. He cannot go snorkeling yet.

This summer, Jamie takes snorkeling lessons. He learns how to breathe through a tube. Then Jamie learns how to swim with flippers. The flippers help him kick better and faster. Finally, Jamie's mom and dad help him practice. For the first time, Jamie gets to snorkel and see the colorful fish.

1. What is the topic of the selection?

_____

2. What is the main idea of the selection?

_____

3. Why can't Jamie go snorkeling at first?

_____

4. What three things does Jamie do in order to snorkel?

_____

_____

_____

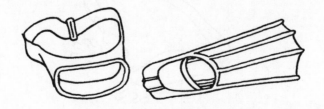

Home Activity Your child found the topic and main idea of a selection. Then your child answered questions that required understanding the details about the main idea. Write a story with your child about a problem you had and how you solved it. Then ask your child to tell the story's topic and main idea.

© Pearson Education 3

Main Idea and Details

The **topic** is what a piece of writing is about. The **main idea** is the most important idea about the **topic**. **Supporting details** are small pieces of information about the **main idea**.

Directions Read the following passage.

> What is the life cycle of a frog? There are three stages.
>
> A frog begins as an egg. The egg hatches in about a week. A small tadpole wiggles out.
>
> A tadpole looks a bit like a fish. It swims around in water, looking for algae to eat.
>
> As the tadpole eats, it grows and changes. The tadpole loses its tail and grows hind legs.
>
> Soon the tadpole is a frog. Now it can hop on land and catch insects with its long tongue.

Directions Complete the graphic organizer to organize the information you read.

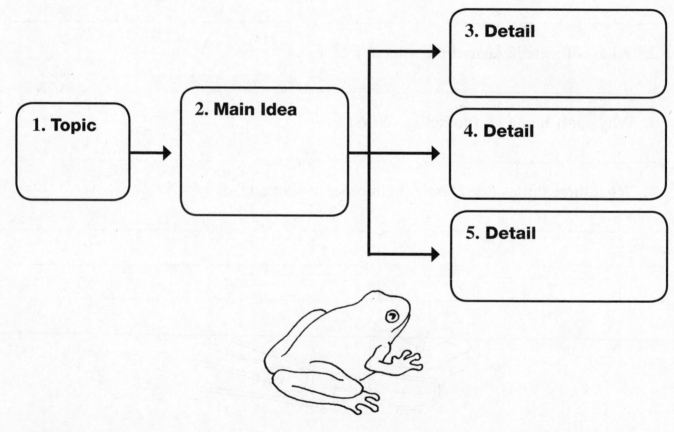

1. Topic

2. Main Idea

3. Detail

4. Detail

5. Detail

© Pearson Education 3

 Home Activity Your child found the topic, main idea, and details in a passage. Talk about an animal your child is familiar with, such as a family pet. Then ask your child what topic you have been talking about (family pet). Ask your child to list three details from your conversation.

Syllables V/CV, VC/V

Directions Circle each word in the box with the **long vowel** sound in the **first syllable**. Underline each word in the box with the **short vowel** sound in the **first syllable**. Then write each word in the correct column.

> | lady | lemon | finish | baby | robot |
> | panel | spider | polish | moment | credit |

long vowel

1. _____

2. _____

3. _____

4. _____

5. _____

short vowel

6. _____

7. _____

8. _____

9. _____

10. _____

Directions Circle each word in the box with the **long vowel** sound in the **first syllable**. Underline each word in the box with the **short vowel** sound in the **first syllable**. Then use the words to complete the sentences. Write each word on the line.

> | menu | female | motor | cousin | zebra |

_____ 11. A _____ horse is called a mare.

_____ 12. A _____ has black and white stripes.

_____ 13. A _____ is a list of food.

_____ 14. Your _____ is your aunt or uncle's child.

_____ 15. A _____ is an engine.

Home Activity Your child identified words that have a long or short vowel sound in the first syllable. Ask your child to read the long and short vowel words he or she circled or underlined on the page above. Help your child use some of these words to write a story.

Dictionary

A **dictionary** is a book of words and their meanings. The words are listed in alphabetical order. **Guide words** are printed in large, dark type at the top of each dictionary page. They show the first and last words printed on the page.

Directions Use the dictionary page to answer the questions.

romp • roost

rook, *n.*
1 a European bird about the size of a crow that lives in a flock with many other birds
2 a cheat
3 *v.* to cheat or trick someone

rookery, *n.* a breeding place for certain animals or birds, such as seals or penguins

rookie, *n.* a beginner, as on a police force or in a sport

1. Which word can be used to describe a football player playing his or her first season?

_____

2. Which entry word or words can be used as a verb?

_____

3. Find the entry word *rook*. Which meaning (1, 2, or 3) of rook is used in this sentence? *The rook flew above the flock.*

_____

4. What are the guide words for this page?

_____

5. Which of these words would be found on this dictionary page: *round, roll, roof, rock*?

_____

© Pearson Education 3

 Home Activity Your child read entries in a dictionary and used them to answer questions. Read a book with your child and have him or her identify two or three unfamiliar words. Ask your child to find the meanings of the words in a dictionary.

Family Times

Summary

A Day's Work

Francisco's grandfather is a carpenter who has arrived from Mexico only two days ago. He wants to work. Francisco wants to help his grandfather. So when a man in a gardening truck comes looking for help for a day, Francisco eagerly promises him the help he needs. He doesn't tell the gardener that his grandfather does not know anything about gardening. Francisco and his grandfather do a beautiful job at their work—except for one big error. They mix up the weeds and the plants, and pull out the wrong plants. Francisco's grandfather makes everything all right, but only after teaching Francisco an important lesson about telling the truth.

Activity

What Can We Do Together? Together, decide on a task that needs to be done around the home. Maybe a fence needs painting, or a leaky faucet needs fixing. Research how to do the job, gather the needed materials, and talk as you go about how to do the best job possible for even the simplest tasks. Then talk about how doing the job together makes it more fun.

Comprehension Skill

Character

A **character** is a person or animal who takes part in the events of a story. Look at what a character says and does to learn what he or she is like.

Activity

Lend a Hand Interview someone who does volunteer work and ask questions such as: *What is the best part about helping? How much time do you give? Is it fun or hard work? Why do you volunteer?* Then discuss with your family how you might help a family member or friend with a messy or unpleasant task.

Words to Know

Knowing the meanings of these words is important to reading *A Day's Work*. Practice using these words.

Vocabulary Words

excitement the state of stirred up emotions

gardener a person who works in or takes care of a garden

motioned directed by wave of hand or another gesture

sadness a state of sorrow or regret

shivered shook, trembled

shocked surprised or horrified

slammed thrown loudly with force

Singular and Plural Nouns

Words that name one person, place, or thing are called **singular nouns.** Words that name more than one are called **plural nouns.** Many plural nouns end in *-s*. Add *-es* to singular nouns that end in *ch, sh, x, s,* or *ss* to make them plural. Some singular nouns end in a consonant and then *y*. To form the plural of these nouns, change the *y* to *i* and add *-es*.

camp	camps	fox	foxes
batch	batches	glass	glasses
ash	ashes	fly	flies

Activity

Back and Forth The first player offers a singular or plural noun. The second player changes it so that a singular noun becomes plural or a plural noun becomes singular.

Singular	Plural	Singular	Plural
cat	cats	bench	benches
toy	toys	lady	ladies
crash	crashes	tax	taxes

Practice Tested Spelling Words

_____ _____ _____ _____

_____ _____ _____ _____

_____ _____ _____ _____

_____ _____ _____ _____

Character • Visualize

- **Characters** are the people or animals in a story. What they say and do tells you about them.
- When you read how a character acts, picture him or her. **Visualizing** will help you understand what the character is like.

Directions Read the following passage.

Missy joined Dee and Karen to write a report on butterflies. "Let's each take one part," said Missy. "I will write about butterfly migration."

But when it was time to meet again, Missy hadn't done her work. Dee and Karen wrote the report without her.

"I know how to make a good cover," said Missy. She took the report. She folded the papers in half. She slipped the papers into an envelope.

"That's not a good cover," said Dee and Karen. Dee and Karen had to make another cover for their report.

Directions Tell about Missy as you complete the graphic organizer.

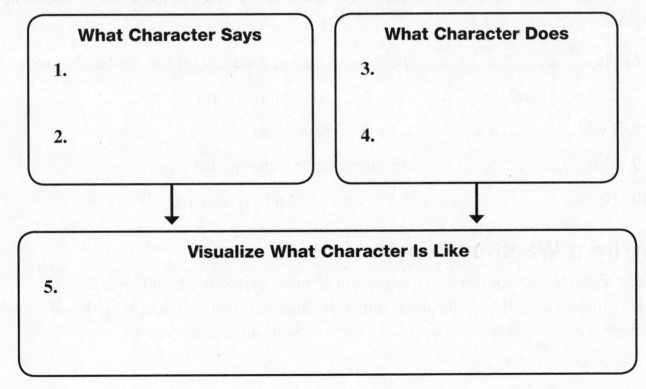

What Character Says

1.

2.

What Character Does

3.

4.

Visualize What Character Is Like

5.

Home Activity Your child answered questions about a story's character. The author reveals information about characters through what a character says and does. Have your child think of other familiar stories. Ask your child to tell what each character is like and why. Your child should be able to support answers with details from the stories.

Vocabulary

Directions Match the word with its meaning. Draw a line from the word to its definition.

> ## Check the Words You Know
>
> ___shivered   ___excitement
> ___motioned   ___shocked
> ___slammed   ___sadness
> ___gardener

1. shivered   surprised

2. shocked   someone who plants and takes care of growing things

3. sadness   trembled or shook

4. motioned   unhappiness

5. gardener   made a move to someone

Directions Choose a word from the box that fits the meaning of the sentence and write it on the line.

6. He _____ the door so hard, a glass fell off the shelf and broke.

7. You could feel the _____ before the race started.

8. I was _____ by the messy room.

9. The _____ trimmed the branches on the bush.

10. He _____ to me with his hand to come and talk to him.

Write a Weather Report

On a separate sheet of paper, write a weather report that tells what the weather is likely to be during the spring and summer. Include information about rainfall and temperature. Use as many vocabulary words as you can in your writing.

© Pearson Education 3

School + Home

Home Activity Your child identified and used new vocabulary words from *A Day's Work*. Read a story about work with your child. Talk about the story using this week's vocabulary words.

Vocabulary • Context Clues

- Sometimes you can figure out the meaning of a word by looking at the words and sentences around it.
- **Context clues** are the words around an unfamiliar word that help you figure out its meaning.

Directions Read the following passage about a garden. Then answer the questions below. Look for context clues as you read.

We used to live in the city. Then we had to move to the country. I was filled with sadness to leave my friends. But I was not unhappy for long. My excitement grew as we drove because I was thrilled to see new things.

It was night when we got to our new house. I got out of the car. It was so cold outside, I shivered. Inside the house, I stopped shaking but was shocked by how dark it was.

"Don't look so surprised," Mom said. "It will look better in the morning."

The next morning, I got up early and went downstairs. Dad was standing by the back door. He raised his arm and motioned for me to follow him outside. There was a beautiful, big garden! It had trees and lots of flowers.

"Can I take care of the garden?" I asked.

"Yes," Dad said, "you can be the family gardener."

I smiled and knew that I would love living in the country.

1. What does *sadness* mean in this passage? What clues help you find out?

_____

2. What does *excitement* mean in this passage? What clues help you find out?

_____

3. What does *shivered* mean in this passage? What clues help you find out?

_____

4. What does *shocked* mean in this passage? What clues help you find out?

_____

5. What does *motioned* mean in this passage? What clues help you find out?

_____

6. What does *gardener* mean in this passage? What clues help you find out?

_____

Home Activity Your child identified and used context clues to understand new words in a passage. Work with your child to identify unfamiliar words in an article and to find context clues to help with understanding new words. Confirm the meanings with your child.

Realism and Fantasy

A **realistic** story tells things that could happen. A **fantasy** story could never happen.

Directions Read the following passage. Then answer the questions below.

There was much excitement in the rental shop. The twins, Jane and James, were at a ski lodge in the mountains. They would ski for the first time!

The twins hobbled out to the ski slope as they shivered in their jackets.

A ski instructor motioned for the twins to come over so she could show them how to use the poles, make turns, and keep their balance. Then the twins took the lift up to an easy hill.

"Let's ski down together," said Jane as she pulled her ski cap tightly around her face.

The twins had just taken off down the slope when suddenly Jane slammed into James. Shocked, both twins fell down.

"Watch where you're going!" said James.

"Maybe we shouldn't ski so close together after all," Jane replied.

1. How do you know that people go skiing in real life?

_____

2. Would James yell at his sister in a realistic story?

_____

3. Does anything happen in this story that could not happen in real life?

_____

4. Is this story a realistic story or a fantasy?

_____

5. Picture the twins running into each other. Tell how you know that this could happen in real life.

_____

 Home Activity Your child answered questions to determine whether a story was realistic or a fantasy. A story is realistic if nothing happens in it that could not happen in real life. Ask similar questions when you read stories together. Have your child explain the answer using prior knowledge.

Character • Visualize

- **Characters** are the people or animals in a story. What they say and do tells you about them.
- When you read how a character acts, picture him or her. **Visualizing** will help you understand what the character is like.

Directions Read the following passage. Then answer the questions below.

Jasmine and Kim play soccer whenever they can. Sometimes they even play on the street in front of their apartment. One Saturday, Jasmine kicked the ball too far, and it went right through a window on the first floor.

"Run!" said Jasmine. "We don't want anyone to find out who did that!"

"But our ball is inside," said Kim. "Everyone will know it was us."

The two girls told the manager what happened. "You must pay for the window," she said, "and then everything will be all right."

1. How do you know that the two girls love soccer?

_____

2. What does Jasmine want to do when the ball goes through the window?

_____

3. Tell what each character is like.

_____

_____

4. Do you think the girls will pay for the broken window? Tell why or why not.

_____

5. Picture the girls talking to the manager. Tell how they probably felt.

_____

Home Activity Your child answered questions about characters in a story. Read a familiar story together and ask your child to tell about the characters based on their actions in the story.

© Pearson Education 3

Character

Characters are the people or animals in a story. What they say and do tells you about them.

Directions Read the following passage.

> "Let's all play baseball at recess," said Jed. So we got the bats and balls. We took them out to the playground. Jed helped us divide into two teams.
>
> "What base do you want to play?" Jed asked Maria.
>
> "I'd rather play in the outfield," Maria said.
>
> So Maria played in the outfield. Jed pitched, like he always does. He struck out several players. No one minded because Jed let everyone play ball.

Directions Tell about Jed as you complete the graphic organizer.

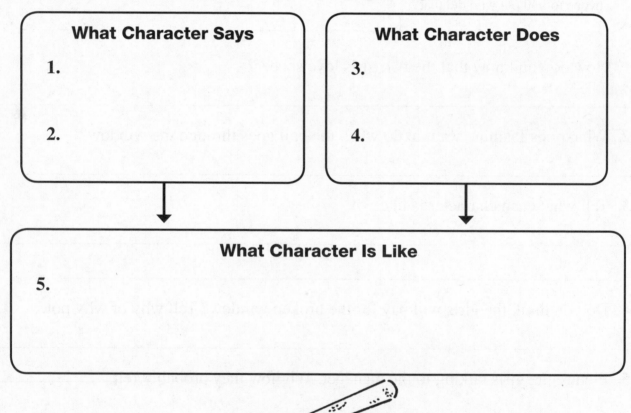

What Character Says

1.

2.

What Character Does

3.

4.

What Character Is Like

5.

Home Activity Your child answered questions about a character from a story. The author reveals information about characters through what a character says and does. Read stories to your child. Ask your child to name the characters in the story. Then ask your child to tell what each character is like, and why. Your child should be able to support his or her answers using details from the story.

© Pearson Education 3

Name _____

Syllables C + *le*

Directions Write the two syllables that make up each word on the lines.

1. _____ + _____ = giggle

2. _____ + _____ = middle

3. _____ + _____ = title

4. _____ + _____ = needle

5. _____ + _____ = marble

6. _____ + _____ = eagle

7. _____ + _____ = bubble

8. _____ + _____ = saddle

9. _____ + _____ = candle

10. _____ + _____ = turtle

Directions Choose the word in the box that matches each picture. Write the word on the line. Then draw a line to divide it into its syllables.

| table   poodle   puzzle   rattle   cattle |

11. _____

12. _____

13. _____

14. _____

15. _____

Home Activity Your child wrote words that end with the final syllable sound heard in *handle*. Help your child make a list of ten more words that end with *-le* (such as *little*, *juggle*, and *nibble*). Work with your child to write a silly poem using some of the *-le* words from your child's list and from the page above.

Procedures and Instructions

Procedures and **instructions** tell the reader how to do or make something.

Directions   Use the instructions for planting a shrub to answer the questions.

Planting a Shrub

1. Use a shovel to dig a hole. The hole should be as deep as the shrub container and twice as wide.

2. Add peat moss to the soil you dig out.

3. Put the shrub (still in the container) in the hole. The top of the container should match the ground.

4. Remove the shrub from the container and place the shrub in the hole.

5. Fill the hole with soil and peat moss.

6. Water the planted shrub thoroughly.

1. What tool do you need to plant the shrub?

_____

2. What do you do with the soil dug from the hole?

_____

3. Why do you put the shrub in the hole when it is still in the container?

_____

4. What do you do after removing the shrub from the container?

_____

5. What is the last thing you do?

_____

© Pearson Education 3

Home Activity Your child answered questions about procedures and instructions. Look through an instruction manual you have and discuss what kind of information it gives the reader.

Family Times

Summary

Prudy's Problem and How She Solved It

Prudy has a collection. Her problem is that it is a collection of everything anyone could possibly collect. It is taking over her house. It is taking over her life. Prudy is forced to come up with a solution. She decides to build an enormous museum for all her collections. The project is wildly successful, and she happily continues to collect and display her treasures.

Activity

One Man's Trash Does your family have collections of things it never meant to collect? This week throw away or donate things taking up space in your home. Spend time in one room of your home, tossing trash and setting aside things that can be donated. Discuss how it feels to have a home with less clutter.

Comprehension Skill

Main Idea and Supporting Details

The **main idea** tells what the story is all about. **Details** are small pieces of information. When you put them all together, they help you understand the main idea.

Activity

String Them Along Write a detail related to a main idea on a paper strip. Together, place the strips of paper into an order that makes sense to you. What main idea do they reflect? Fill in missing details on new paper strips. Then use glue or tape to make a paper strip loop. Thread the loops together to make a chain.

Lesson Vocabulary

Words to Know

Knowing the meanings of these words is important to reading *Prudy's Problem*. Practice using these words.

Vocabulary Words

collection a gathering of items that are similar in some way

enormous very large; huge

realize to understand clearly

scattered spread about in various places

shiny bright and polished

strain to draw too tight; stretch too much

Grammar

Irregular Plural Nouns

An **irregular plural noun** is not spelled by adding *-s* or *-es* to the singular. For example, the plural of *man* is not *mans* but *men*. Irregular plural nouns must be learned because they do not follow the regular rules.

Activity

Matching Write the noun pairs below on index cards. Mix the cards and put them facedown in rows. Players take turns flipping over two cards and reading the words. If the words name the same noun in the singular and plural, the player keeps the pair. If the cards don't refer to the same person, place, or thing, then the cards are turned facedown, and play goes to the next player.

man	men	woman	women
child	children	mouse	mice
foot	feet	tooth	teeth
leaf	leaves	life	lives

Practice Tested Spelling Words

_____ _____ _____ _____

_____ _____ _____ _____

_____ _____ _____ _____

_____ _____ _____ _____

Main Idea • Monitor and Fix Up

- The **main idea** answers the question, "What is this story all about?" **Details** are small pieces of information that help tell what the story is about.

- As you read, ask yourself, "What are the important details in this story so far?" **Sum up** to help you understand what is happening and to help you tell what the story is about.

Directions Read the following passage.

Kendra saw all sorts of colorful rocks at the beach. She had been looking for something to collect. Kendra decided she would collect rocks.

Kendra loaded her backpack with red rocks, yellow rocks, black rocks, and speckled rocks. Then she lugged them home.

Once home, Kendra looked for a place to keep her rocks. She couldn't keep them in her backpack.

Kendra found a pretty box. She set the colorful rocks in the box and put them on the porch.

Kendra showed her beautiful rock collection to everyone who came to visit.

Directions Complete the graphic organizer to tell what the story is all about.

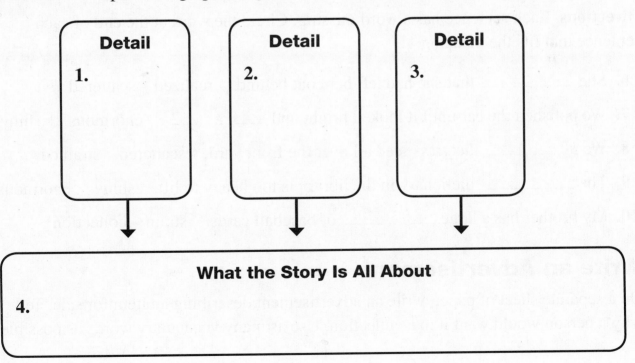

Detail

1.

Detail

2.

Detail

3.

What the Story Is All About

4.

School + Home

Home Activity Your child found the main idea of a story. The main idea is a sentence that sums up what the story is all about. Read a story like the one above, and ask your child to name some of the details in the story and then write one sentence to tell what the story is all about.

Vocabulary

Directions Choose the vocabulary word from the box and write it next to its meaning.

Check the Words You Know

___enormous   ___shiny
___strain   ___scattered
___collection   ___realize

_____ 1. spread over a large area

_____ 2. a group of similar things a person gets and saves

_____ 3. to understand something clearly

_____ 4. to stretch too much

_____ 5. very big; huge

Directions Each sentence has a word missing. Circle the word at the end of each sentence that fits the meaning.

6. She _____ that she had left her coat behind.   realized   scattered

7. We polished the car until it looked bright and _____.   enormous   shiny

8. We _____ the grass seed all over the front yard.   scattered   strained

9. The _____ dictionary in the library is too heavy to lift.   shiny   enormous

10. My brother has a large _____ of baseball cards.   strain   collection

Write an Advertisement

On a separate sheet of paper, write an advertisement describing an item for sale. Tell why a person would want it in a collection. Use as many vocabulary words as possible.

Home Activity Your child identified and used vocabulary words from *Prudy's Problem and How She Solved It*. Ask your child to explain Prudy's problem to you and how it was solved. Encourage your child to use as many vocabulary words as possible.

Vocabulary • Dictionary

- Sometimes when you are reading, you come across a word you don't know. You can use a **dictionary** to find the meaning of the word.
- A **dictionary** has word meanings. The words are listed in alphabetical order.

clutter *n.* mess
collection *n.* a group of similar things one
    gets and keeps
organize *v.* to put in order

realize *v.* to come to see; to understand
scrutinize *v.* to look very closely at; to study
vacuum *n.* machine used to take dirt from
    floors, rugs, and carpets

Directions Each sentence has one underlined word. Use the dictionary entries above to find the meaning.

1. Mom told me to <u>organize</u> all the things in my room.

  _____

2. Every Saturday morning, Dad uses a <u>vacuum</u> on the rugs in the house.

  _____

3. There is so much <u>clutter</u> in my closet, I can't find anything.

  _____

4. My room looks clean as long as you don't <u>scrutinize</u> it.

  _____

5. Now I keep each of my <u>collections</u> in a separate box.

  _____

6. I <u>realize</u> that having too many things can sometimes make life difficult.

  _____

Home Activity Your child used sample dictionary entries to find the meaning of unfamiliar words. Read a story or newspaper article together and look up unfamiliar words. Encourage your child to identify unfamiliar words while reading and then look up their definitions in a dictionary.

Character

Characters are the people or animals in the story. What they say and do tells you about them.

Directions Read the following passage. Then answer the questions below.

A group of gophers had an inspiration. They gathered together a huge collection of leaves. It was a strain to carry them into their holes. But gophers need bedding to sleep on during the winter, and those leaves were perfect.

While they worked, an enormous moose with a shiny nose came by.

"What's all this clutter?" the moose demanded as he scattered the leaves with his big feet.

Phil, a grandfather gopher, spoke up. "For your information, we use leaves for bedding in the winter," he said.

"Oh, I'm sorry," said the moose. "I didn't realize what you were doing."

1. How do you know that the gophers are hardworking?

_____

_____

2. What word would you use to describe the moose when he first shows up?

_____

3. What word would you use to describe Phil?

_____

4. Why does the moose say that he is sorry?

_____

_____

5. Think about how you felt about the moose when he first showed up.
Then think about how you felt about him at the end of the story.
Tell how your feelings about the moose changed, and why.

Home Activity Your child answered questions about the characters in a story. Read a new story together. As you read, stop occasionally and name a character. Ask what that character has said or done so far and have your child name words that describe the character.

Main Idea • Monitor and Fix Up

- The **main idea** can be found by asking, "What is this story all about? **Details** are small pieces of information that help tell what the story is about.

- As you read, ask yourself, "What are the important details so far?" **Sum up** to help you understand what is happening and to help you tell what the story is about.

Directions Read the following passage. Then answer the questions below.

> Jermaine's bedroom was so full of books that they covered the bed, and Jermaine had nowhere to sleep.
>
> "I need to do something about this," thought Jermaine. So he found some old bricks and boards in the garden.
>
> Jermaine took all the books out of his bedroom. He laid bricks on the floor up against the walls and stacked a board on top.
>
> Then Jermaine put down more bricks and stacked another board on top. Jermaine repeated the steps many more times. Soon Jermaine had bookshelves that went to the ceiling, and all of Jermaine's books fit on the shelves.

1. What details in the first paragraph will help you tell what this story is all about?

_____

2. Jermaine decides he needs to do something about the books. How does this detail help you understand what this story is all about?

_____

_____

3. The bookshelves went to the ceiling. Is this an important detail? Explain.

_____

_____

4. Use the details to sum up. Tell what this story is all about.

_____

Home Activity Your child used details in a story to determine its main idea, or what the story is all about. Have your child recall familiar stories. Discuss the important details. Then help your child write a sentence to tell what the story is all about.

Main Idea

The **main idea** answers the question, "What is this story all about?" **Details** are small pieces of information that help tell what the story is about.

Directions Read the following passage.

John went into the woods on a snowy day, and his boots made tracks where he walked.

"I can follow my tracks back out," thought John, so he didn't pay attention to where he was going.

But the sun came out and melted the snow, and when John wanted to leave, he couldn't see any tracks.

Then John saw an eagle overhead. "Eagle," said John. "Please help me find my way out."

The eagle flew south, then west. John followed until he was out of the woods.

Directions Complete the graphic organizer to tell what the story is all about.

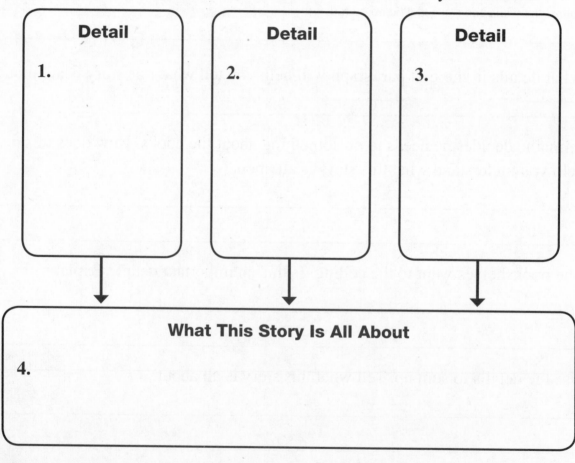

Detail

1.

Detail

2.

Detail

3.

What This Story Is All About

4.

© Pearson Education 3

 Home Activity Your child found the main idea of a story. The main idea is a sentence that sums up what the story is all about. Read a story like the one above with your child. Ask your child to name details from the story and then tell what the story is all about.

78 Comprehension

Practice Book Unit 2

Compound Words

Directions Identify the two words that make up each compound word. Write the words on the lines.

1. _____ + _____ = sunglasses

2. _____ + _____ = railroad

3. _____ + _____ = haircut

4. _____ + _____ = firehouse

5. _____ + _____ = popcorn

6. _____ + _____ = myself

7. _____ + _____ = greenhouse

8. _____ + _____ = backyard

9. _____ + _____ = rainwater

10. _____ + _____ = sunflower

Directions Choose the compound word to complete each sentence. Write the word on the line. Draw a line between the two words that make up each compound word.

_____ 11. My (grandfather/uncle) lives on a farm.

_____ 12. I help him take care of his animals (whenever/when) I visit.

_____ 13. Last winter I was with him during a terrible (snowstorm/blizzard).

_____ 14. We had to work (outside/quickly) in the cold and snow.

_____ 15. It's (sometimes/often) difficult to be a farmer.

Home Activity Your child wrote compound words—words formed by joining two shorter words—such as *homework*. With your child, read advertisements to find compound words (such as *everyday, something,* and *everyone*). Have your child identify the two words that make up each compound word.

© Pearson Education 3

Magazine or Periodical

Directions Read the magazine article. Use it to answer the questions below.

Collector's Monthly	
How to Manage Your Collectibles *By Sara Vega* We all love our collectibles, but often there are too many items to manage. Here are some suggestions: • Set a goal or purpose for your collection. Get rid of items that don't meet this goal or purpose. • Buy or make storage containers. You want to be able to view each item. • Make a list of each item in your collection. Add and remove items from the list as needed. You may want to keep your list on a computer.	**FOR SALE** **Action Figures** More than 100 favorites. Call Mike 430-1874. **Rare Coins** Many hard-to-find U.S. coins. 555-7372 Ask for Marcia.

1. What is the title of the magazine?

_____

2. What is the title of the article?

_____

3. What is the article about?

_____

_____

4. Who might buy this magazine?

_____

_____

5. If you were looking for a rare coin or sports card, how might you use this magazine?

_____

_____

Home Activity Your child read a magazine page and answered questions about it. Look through a children's magazine. Ask your child to point out the different parts. Have him or her suggest other articles or materials that might be found in a magazine like this.

Family Times

Summary

Tops and Bottoms

Bear is an animal with a lot of land, a lot of money, and absolutely no get-up-and-go. Left to his own devices, he can sleep through anything. Hare is a clever rabbit who didn't always make the best decisions in the past. He now has a big family, no land, and no food. He tricks Bear into letting him farm his land. By the end of their "business deal," both Bear and Hare have learned that good things come through hard work.

Activity

What Could You Do? Imagine you have a need for something such as a new pair of sports shoes or school clothes. What can you do to earn those things? Brainstorm jobs that you can do together that would help someone else as you earn money. For example, your family might offer to rake leaves in your neighborhood for a fee. How is the work different when you do it together?

Comprehension Skill

Author's Purpose

The **author's purpose** is the reason an author writes something. An author writes to persuade, to inform, to entertain, or to express ideas and feelings.

Activity

Book Talk Have each participant bring a favorite book to present. Take turns telling the title, the author, and a little about what happens in the story. Then tell what you think the author's purpose was in writing the story. Finally, trade books with someone who had a book you think sounded interesting or fun. Spend some time reading.

Lesson Vocabulary

Words to Know

Knowing the meanings of these words is important to reading *Tops and Bottoms*. Practice using these words.

Vocabulary Words

bottom the lowest part

cheated acted dishonestly

clever having a quick mind

crops plants grown to be used as food or sold for profit

lazy not willing to work

partners people who run a business together and share the gains and losses of it

wealth a great amount of money or valuable things

Grammar

Singular Possessive Nouns

To show that one person owns something, use a **singular possessive noun.** Add an apostrophe and the letter *s* (*'s*) to a singular noun to make it a singular possessive noun.

Activity
To Whom Does This Belong?

Write singular nouns on index cards. On one card, write *'s* and trim the card so that the *'s*, when placed at the end of any of the other cards, will make the word possessive. Next, mix the word cards. Each player chooses a card. Players then take turns placing the *'s* card on their word card, reading the new singular possessive noun aloud, and then saying a sentence using that singular possessive noun.

Practice Tested Spelling Words

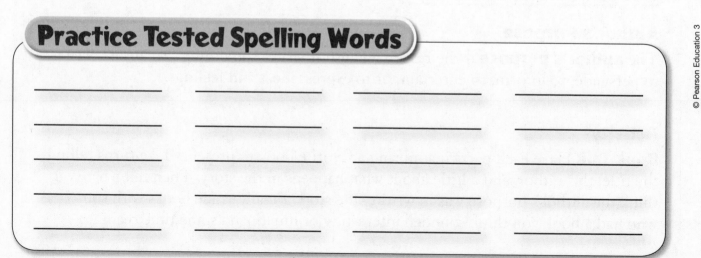

Author's Purpose • Predict

- The **author's purpose** is the reason an author writes something. Some reasons are to inform or teach, to entertain, to persuade, or to express ideas and feelings.
- Good readers try to **predict** what will happen and why. You can also **predict** the **author's purpose**.

Directions Read the passage and follow the directions to complete the graphic organizer.

Planting Bushes

STOP and answer Question 1 below.
The Lopez family had just built a nice house in the desert. The only problem was that the hot sun shone through the huge windows on the south side.

Early one morning, Dad and Grandpa planted bushes along the south side of the house.

"I wonder why they did that," thought Lupe.

STOP and answer Question 2 below.
Every day, Dad or Grandpa watered the bushes. They began to grow. Soon the bushes got so tall they blocked the sun from coming in the windows.

"Now I know why they did that!" thought Lupe.

---

1. Before You Read: Read the title. For which reason might the author write a passage with this title?

⬇

2. As You Read: Predict the author's purpose. Why do you think the author is telling this story?

⬇

3. After You Read: Give the author's purpose. Why did the author most likely write this selection? Explain.

Home Activity Your child determined the author's purpose for writing a story. Purposes include to inform, to persuade, to entertain, or to express feelings or ideas. Talk about the author's purpose for writing tales your child is familiar with. Ask your child to give reasons for his or her answers.

© Pearson Education 3

Vocabulary

Directions Each sentence has an underlined word. Circle the word at the end of the sentence with the same meaning as the underlined word.

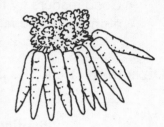

Check the Words You Know
___lazy ___bottom
___crops ___clever
___cheated ___partners
___wealth

1. My <u>lazy</u> brother hates to do his chores.   idle   young

2. Jill put the cookies on the <u>bottom</u> shelf.   lowest   long

3. Juan and I are <u>partners</u> in a lawn mowing business.   co-workers   a class

4. Jim does well in school because he is very <u>clever</u>.   lazy   smart

5. A person with lots of money has lots of <u>wealth</u>.   riches   need

Directions Write a word from the box to complete each sentence below.

6. The farmer plants many _____ , including corn and wheat.

7. A farmer cannot be _____ because farming takes lots of work.

8. Ann is an honest student, so I don't think she _____ on the test.

9. The rich man had so much _____ , he owned five houses.

10. We will work together as _____ to build a business.

Write a Story

On a separate sheet of paper, write about two farmers working together on something special. Describe them and what happens. Use as many vocabulary words as possible.

© Pearson Education 3

School + Home **Home Activity** Your child identified and used vocabulary words from *Tops and Bottoms*. Visit the supermarket produce aisle together and have your child identify the vegetables whose tops or bottoms we eat. Encourage using as many vocabulary words as possible.

Vocabulary • Context Clues

- Sometimes you come across a word you don't know. The author may use a word with the opposite meaning—an **antonym**—as a clue to the word's meaning.
- Use **antonyms** as **context clues** to figure out the meaning of unfamiliar words.

Directions Read each sentence. One word is underlined. Circle the antonym of the underlined word. Write the meaning of the underlined word on the line.

1. Sue is always so busy that no one can say she is <u>lazy</u>.

_____

2. Put the glass on the top shelf because your sister may break it if it's on the <u>bottom</u>.

_____

3. Danny is so <u>clever</u>, he would never do a silly thing like that.

_____

4. The cat was <u>asleep</u>, but the dog was awake.

_____

5. Months after planting the seeds, the farmer can <u>harvest</u> the corn.

_____

6. Do not scatter the papers, but <u>gather</u> them into one pile.

_____

7. You look so nice when you smile that you should never <u>scowl</u>.

_____

8. Whisper the secret in my ear, don't <u>holler</u> it out loud.

_____

Home Activity Your child identified and used new words by understanding antonyms used in context. Read a story together and encourage identifying unfamiliar words. Then help look for antonyms in the text that might help figure out the words' meanings.

Main Idea and Details

The **main idea** answers the question, "What is this story all about?" **Details** are small pieces of information that help tell what the story is about.

Directions Read the following passage. Then answer the questions below.

Two pigs were hungry for corn, so they decided to plant some at the bottom of a hill. Mr. Pigg planted the crops while Mr. Hogg watered them. When it was time to pick the corn, the two partners worked together.

"We have a ton of corn," said Mr. Pigg when they were done. "Let's share our wealth with our neighbors."

The neighbors were delighted.

"What clever farmers you are," said Mrs. Hoof.

"You sure aren't lazy," said Mrs. Barnyard.

After that, the two pigs grew corn every summer. In the fall, they shared what they harvested.

1. What is the topic of this story?

_____

2. What lesson could the reader learn from this story?

_____

3. What is this story all about?

_____

4. Do you think the two pigs will continue to share their harvest? Explain.

_____

_____

© Pearson Education 3

School + Home **Home Activity** Your child answered questions about the story's main idea. What the story is all about often has to do with a lesson the reader can learn from reading it. Read animal fables together. Talk about what the animals learn and what the reader can learn. Then ask your child to write a sentence stating the fable's main idea.

Author's Purpose • Predict

- **Author's purpose** is the reason an author writes something. Some reasons are to inform or teach, to entertain, to persuade, or to express ideas and feelings.
- Good readers try to **predict** what will happen and why. You can also **predict** the **author's purpose**.

Directions Read the following passage. Then answer the questions below.

Being a Farmer

Farming is a wonderful business. You can raise many animals, from pigs to horses. You can grow many different kinds of crops. You can be your own boss.

Your children will grow up in the country. You can stay in shape by working hard with your hands. You will be surrounded by peace and quiet.

Farmers make money by selling the crops they grow. Some farmers can make good money and enjoy a good life.

1. When you first read the title, what did you think this passage would be about?

_____

2. Why do you think the author wrote this passage?

_____

3. Explain your reasons for choosing the author's purpose.

_____

_____

4. Did the author do a good job of making the reader want to be a farmer? Why or why not?

_____

_____

Home Activity Your child read a story and then answered questions about the author's purpose. After reading stories to your child, stop to discuss why the author may have written the story. Authors write for various reasons. An author may have more than one purpose. Common reasons for writing are to entertain, inform, persuade, or express ideas or feelings.

Author's Purpose

Author's purpose is the reason an author writes something. Some reasons are to inform or teach, to entertain, to persuade, or to express ideas and feelings.

Directions Read the title and answer question 1. Read the first part, and answer question 2. Then finish the passage and complete the graphic organizer.

> **The Cat and the Cherries**
> Cat loved cherries on the trees in the orchard. Bird helped Cat by dropping cherries onto the ground so she could eat them. But today Bird was nowhere in sight. Cat just had to have a cherry!
> Cat clawed her way up the tiny tree. After she feasted on several cherries, she tried to go down. But she couldn't get out of the tree.
> Then Bird flew by. "Why are you in the tree?" he asked.
> "I wanted a cherry," said Cat. "But now I can't get down."
> "You should have waited for your friend to help you," said Bird.

1. Before You Read: Read the title. For which reason might the author write a story with this title?

2. As You Read: Predict the author's purpose. Why do you think the author is telling this story?

3. After You Read: Now what do you think the author's purpose was?

Home Activity Your child read a story and then determined the author's purpose. Read a fairy tale or fable to your child. Discuss reasons why the author may have written the story. If your child needs help, ask if the story teaches, entertains, persuades, or expresses ideas or feelings.

© Pearson Education 3

Consonant Blends

Directions Read the story. Underline the words with the three-letter blends **spl, squ, str,** and **thr**. Then write the underlined words on the lines.

Emily threw on her coat and ran down the street. As she got to the town square, she saw three friends throwing water balloons at one another. Each time a balloon struck the ground, it split open. Water splashed everywhere. Then someone tossed a balloon with such strength that it flew through an open car window. Emily knew they had to find the owner and tell what they had done.

1. _____

2. _____

3. _____

4. _____

5. _____

6. _____

7. _____

8. _____

9. _____

10. _____

Directions Read each word and listen for the three-letter blend. Then write two more words that start with the same blend. Underline the three-letter blend in each word you write.

11. straw _____   _____

12. splurge _____   _____

13. squeak _____   _____

14. thread _____   _____

15. straight _____   _____

Home Activity Your child wrote words that begin with the three-letter blends *spl* (as in *splash*), *squ* (as in *square*), *str* (as in *strike*), and *thr* (as in *throw*). Challenge your child to name additional words that begin with these three-letter blends. For help in identifying words with these starting letters, you can use a dictionary.

© Pearson Education 3

Encyclopedia

An **encyclopedia** is a set of books, or **volumes,** that has **entries** and articles on many subjects. Volumes and entries are arranged in alphabetical order. **Guide words** show the first and last entries on a page or facing pages. **Electronic encyclopedias** display links to articles on subjects for which you search.

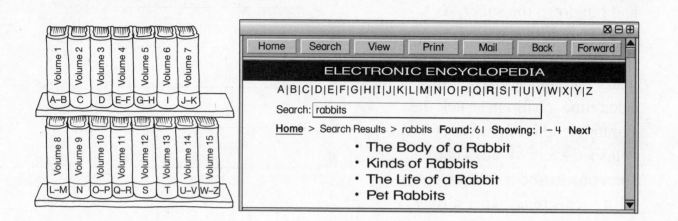

Directions Use the information above to answer the questions.

1. What word or words would you use to find information about the climate of the Northeast United States? Write the volume number you would use.

_____

2. The entry *tortoise* might be found between which guide words: **tidal wave/tiger, tornado/town,** or **toy/trampoline?** Write the volume number in which it would be found.

_____

3. You want to compare an alligator and a crocodile. Which volumes will you use?

_____

4. How many different articles on rabbits are shown in the electronic encyclopedia window? _____

5. Which article will you read to learn about the size of a rabbit?

_____

© Pearson Education 3

Home Activity Your child identified words and volume numbers to locate answers to questions about using an encyclopedia. Help your child write four or five questions about a topic of interest. Have your child use an encyclopedia, either print or electronic, to answer the questions.

Family Times

Summary

William's House

William and his wife have settled in a new land. He builds his family a house exactly like the one he grew up in. But as time passes, he finds that summers are a little warmer, the winds blow harder, and the air turns drier than at home. Each change in the weather prompts William to make a change in his home until it is perfect for his new land.

Activity

Solving Problems Together, take a walk around your home and see it with new eyes. Do you have carpeting? What purpose does it serve? Is there anything your home needs that it doesn't have? How could you work together to make it?

Comprehension Skill

Draw Conclusions

A **conclusion** is a decision you reach after you think about details and facts. As you read, think about the **details** and **facts** and use **what you already know** to better understand the characters and events.

Activity

Widget Whatsit Go to the kitchen area of a store and look at the kitchen gadgets. Together, find any unfamiliar tools. Discuss what you know about cooking and think aloud about the characteristics of the gadget. Is it meant for mixing? for cutting? for high or low temperatures? Draw conclusions about the gadget's use, and then check the packaging to see how the item is meant to be used.

© Pearson Education 3

Words to Know

Knowing the meanings of these words is important to reading *William's House*. Practice using these words.

Vocabulary Words

barrels large, round wooden containers with curved sides

cellar room built underground

clearing a piece of land free of trees and bushes

pegs pieces of wood driven into a surface to hold things

spoil to become bad or not fit to eat or use

steep having a very sharp slope

Grammar

Plural Possessive Nouns

If two or more people share or own something, use a **plural possessive noun.** Add an apostrophe to plural nouns that end in *-s* (*the boys' shirts*), *-es* (*the benches' legs*), or *-ies* (*the ladies' hats*) to make them possessive. Add an apostrophe and an *-s* to make irregular plural nouns possessive (*the men's coats*).

Activity
Using Plural Possessive Nouns

Write sentences similar to the following on paper. Help your child decide the correct way to make the underlined word possessive. Then have your child read aloud the corrected sentences.

1. Put the <u>boys</u> _____ boots by the door.

2. The <u>puppies</u> _____ collars are blue.

3. Are those the <u>children</u> _____ coats?

Practice Tested Spelling Words

_____ _____ _____ _____

_____ _____ _____ _____

_____ _____ _____ _____

_____ _____ _____ _____

_____ _____ _____ _____

Draw Conclusions • Ask Questions

- A **conclusion** is a decision you reach after you think about details and facts. Then think about **what you already know** to help **draw conclusions**.
- As you read, **ask yourself** why certain things happen or why characters act as they do. You may be able to **draw conclusions** about them.

Directions Read the following passage.

The Chumash lived in California long before settlers came. They lived in huge round houses made from tule reeds.

First, the Chumash placed willow poles around a circle. Then they bent the poles and tied them together at the top. The people covered the poles with mats made from reeds. A hole was left in the top of the house.

A house was 50 feet across. Aunts, uncles, and cousins all lived together in one house. A fire burned in the center pit. The rest of the space was divided into areas for each family.

Directions Complete the graphic organizer to draw a conclusion.

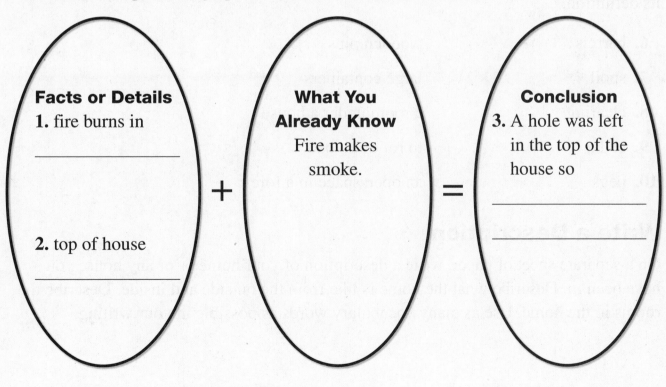

Facts or Details
1. fire burns in
_____

2. top of house
_____

+

What You Already Know
Fire makes smoke.

=

Conclusion
3. A hole was left in the top of the house so
_____
_____

Home Activity Your child used a graphic organizer to draw a conclusion. Authors don't tell the reader everything. Readers draw conclusions while they read to help them understand the story. Reread or retell the story "The Three Little Pigs." Ask your child to tell why each house except the brick house blew down. (They were not strong enough.)

Name _____

Vocabulary

Check the Words You Know

___clearing   ___pegs
___steep   ___cellar
___barrels   ___spoil

Directions Read the sentences. Write the word from the box that fits the sentence.

1. We set up our tent in a _____ in the woods.

2. We put _____ from our tent into the ground to hold it down.

3. The hill was so _____ , I nearly slipped and fell.

4. We keep lots of tools downstairs in our _____ .

5. You must use eggs before they _____ and make you sick.

Directions Match the word with its meaning. Draw a line from the word to its definition.

6. barrels   wooden pins

7. spoil   large containers

8. clearing   a room under a house

9. cellar   to rot or go bad

10. pegs   an open space in a forest

Write a Description

On a separate sheet of paper, write a description of your home or of any house you have been in. Describe what the home is like from the outside and inside. Describe the rooms in the home. Use as many vocabulary words as possible in your writing.

Home Activity Your child identified and used vocabulary words from *William's House*. Ask your child to describe William's house using as many vocabulary words as possible.

© Pearson Education 3

Vocabulary • Context Clues

Sometimes in your reading you see a word you don't know. You can use **context clues**—the words and sentences around the unfamiliar word—to figure out its meaning.

Directions Read the following passage. Then answer the questions.

Last summer, my family and I spent two weeks living in a log cabin. The cabin was in a clearing, where the trees had been cut down. Life in a log cabin is very different from life in the city. You hang your clothes on pegs sticking out of the wall. Even pots and pans hang on pegs in the kitchen. Under the kitchen rug was a trap door. It led downstairs to the cellar.

My brother and I loved the cellar. We had to walk down very steep stairs almost like a ladder! The cellar was filled with large, covered barrels containing dried corn and other food. Also, the cellar was very cool. Food does not spoil where it is cool. So the food in the cellar stayed fresh. The cellar was a great place to be on a hot summer day!

1. What does *clearing* mean in this passage? What clues help you determine the meaning?

_____

_____

2. What does *pegs* mean in this passage? What clues help you determine the meaning?

_____

_____

3. What does *cellar* mean in this passage? What clues help you determine the meaning?

_____

_____

4. What does *steep* mean in this passage? What clues help you determine the meaning?

_____

_____

5. What does *barrels* mean in this passage? What clues help you determine the meaning?

_____

_____

Home Activity Your child identified and used context clues to understand new words in a passage. Work with your child to identify unfamiliar words in a paragraph, then have your child find context clues to help with the understanding of new words. Confirm the meaning with your child.

Character

Characters are the people or animals in a story. What they say and do tells you about them.

Directions Read the following passage. Then answer the questions below.

It was five o'clock in the morning, and Pierre felt someone tapping his shoulder. "Pierre," said Grandpa, "it's time to wake up. The fish are waiting!" Pierre snuggled back into his blanket and thought, *Why are we getting up so early?* He put his head back under the covers.

"I'm ready, Grandpa!" said Pierre's brother Luc. "Let's go!" Luc had woken up extra early to be ready to go when Grandpa arrived. It was a big day. Grandpa had come from far away to take the boys on their first fishing trip to the big river.

Luc and Grandpa set off for the river, while Pierre stayed in bed. They returned at the end of the day with lots of fish and lots of stories.

At dinner, Luc and Grandpa were telling about their day and the fun they shared. Pierre was sad that he had stayed in bed and missed the adventure.

1. Who are the main characters in this story?

_____

2. How do you know that Luc was excited to go fishing?

_____

3. Why is it a big day?

_____

4. Why was Pierre sad at the end of the story?

_____

5. Write a question about why Pierre stayed in bed. Then tell what the answer reveals about Pierre.

_____

_____

_____

© Pearson Education 3

Home Activity Your child answered questions about a story's characters. Clues in the story help the reader decide what a character is like. Understanding what the characters are like will help your child better understand the story. When your child reads stories, ask what the characters are like, and why.

Draw Conclusions • Ask Questions

- A **conclusion** is a decision you reach after you think about details and facts and then think about **what you already know** to help **draw conclusions**.

- As you read, ask yourself why certain things happen or why characters act as they do. You may be able to **draw conclusions** about them.

Directions Read the following passage. Then answer the questions below.

My friends and I formed a game club, but we needed a place to meet. We decided to use some leftover lumber from my backyard to build a tree house. We hauled wood up a ladder to the highest branches, and then we started to pound nails to make the floor.

"What are you doing?" screeched Mom. "Get down!" Fortunately, Dad decided to help us. He got the floorboards straight and secure, and then he put up walls and a roof. Finally, we had our game room.

1. Why do you think the club didn't meet at someone's house?

_____

2. Why do you think Mom wanted the friends to get down?

_____

3. Why might Dad have decided to help the friends?

_____

4. Do you think the following is a valid conclusion? Explain your reasons.

The tree house is a safe tree house.

_____

5. Write a question you might ask about the friends hauling wood up the tree. Then tell how you could use the answer to draw a conclusion.

_____

_____

© Pearson Education 3

Home Activity Your child answered questions that required drawing conclusions. We all draw conclusions as we read by using facts and details in the story and our own experiences. When your child reads, ask questions such as the ones above. Also ask your child to give reasons for any conclusions drawn.

Draw Conclusions

A **conclusion** is a decision you reach after you think about details and facts and then think about **what you already know** to **draw conclusions**.

Directions Read the following passage.

Jane's ancestors moved to Kansas about 150 years ago. They built a sod house. Sod is pieces of earth with grass growing on them.

Pa dug a hole in a hill. Then he cut sod into strips. Pa stacked the sod to make a wall. He left an opening for a door.

To make a roof, Pa laced twigs, branches, and hay together. Then he put

sod on top of that. At night, dirt fell from the ceiling onto Jane as she slept.

Ma cooked inside the sod house. Often, she had to put an umbrella over the pot and over her family as they ate.

Directions Complete the graphic organizer to draw a conclusion.

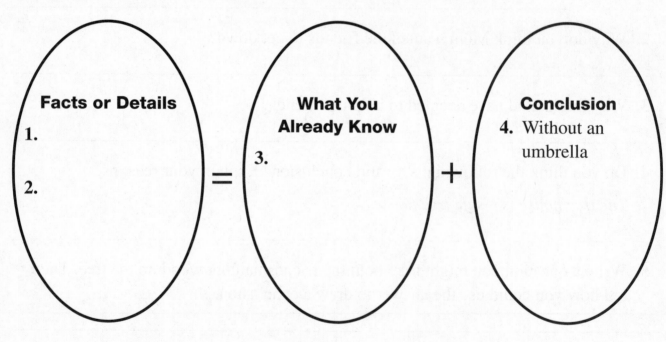

Facts or Details
1.

2.

=

What You Already Know
3.

+

Conclusion
4. Without an umbrella

© Pearson Education 3

Home Activity Your child learned to draw conclusions. A conclusion is a decision that readers make by thinking about the facts and details in a story. Readers draw conclusions all the time as they read. Listen to your child read and ask questions that require him or her to draw conclusions about the characters or events in a story.

Consonant Digraphs

Directions Write **sh, th, ph, ch, tch,** or **ng** to complete each word. Write the whole word on the line to the left.

_____ **1.** Maria's family pur____ased a house.

_____ **2.** Her mo____er decided to paint it.

_____ **3.** She went to the store and bought bru____es and buckets.

_____ **4.** When she came home she put on old clo____ing.

_____ **5.** Then she pa____ed the cracks and nail holes.

_____ **6.** Maria didn't know what color her room was goi____ to be.

_____ **7.** She ____oned her friend to talk about it.

_____ **8.** Her friend helped Maria make the ____oice.

_____ **9.** Maria picked a beautiful ____ade of peach.

Directions Say the name of each picture. Write **sh, th, wh, ph, tch,** or **ng** to complete each word.

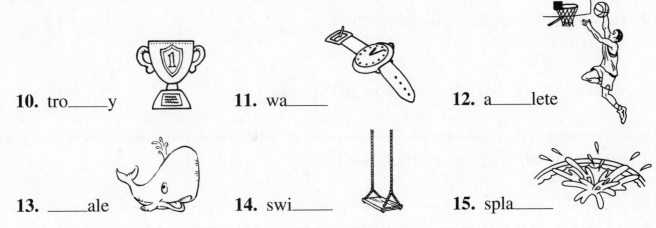

10. tro____y

11. wa____

12. a____lete

13. ____ale

14. swi____

15. spla____

Home Activity Your child wrote words with the consonants *sh (English)*, *th (father)*, *wh (wheel)*, *ph (trophy)*, *ch (chapter)*, *tch (watch)*, and *ng (wing)*. Have your child read the words on the page above. Ask your child to change one or more letters in some of the words to form new words. For example, substituting *t* for *p* in *peach* forms *teach*.

© Pearson Education 3

Diagram

A **diagram** is a special drawing with labels. It usually shows how something is put together, how its parts relate to one another, or how it works. This diagram shows some of the parts of a house.

Diagram

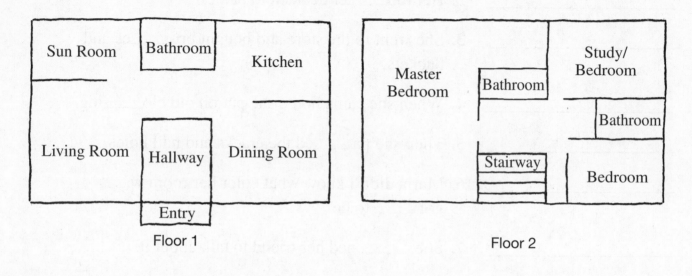

Floor 1   Floor 2

Directions Use the information from the diagram to answer each question.

1. How many floors does this house have?

_____

2. How many rooms are on the second floor?

_____

3. What appears to be the largest room in the house?

_____

4. How many bathrooms does this house have?

_____

5. According to the diagram what room is above the kitchen?

_____

 Home Activity Your child used a diagram to answer questions. Have your child make a drawing of one floor in your home. Encourage him or her to label each room and possibly furniture or other fixtures.

© Pearson Education 3

Family Times

Summary

The Gardener

Lydia Grace goes to live with her uncle in the city when money gets tight at home. She helps in his bakery, learns to make bread, and makes friends there. Lydia loves to garden, and even though gardening space is limited in the city, she makes the best of what room she has. By the end of the story, she has transformed her uncle's building with her passion for growing things.

Activity

Plant a Window Garden Fill a pan with soil. Find seeds suitable for a small space such as herbs for cooking or small flowers. Plant them following the directions on the package. How do the flowers change the feel of the window in which they sit?

Comprehension Skill

Cause and Effect

A **cause** tells why something happened. An **effect** is what happened. Words such as *because*, *since*, and *so* are clues that can help you figure out a cause and its effect.

Activity

Marbles Use marbles or tennis balls to explore cause and effect. What happens when one marble strikes another? Can you make the second marble go in the direction you want? What happens if you try to bounce a marble on the floor? Experiment with cause and effect together.

Lesson Vocabulary

Words to Know

Knowing the meanings of these words is important to reading *The Gardener*. Practice using these words to learn their meanings.

Vocabulary Words

beauty quality that makes a person or thing pleasing to look at

blooming the opening of flowers on a plant

bulbs the round parts of some plants that are underground

doze to sleep lightly or for a short time

humor the ability to enjoy funny things

recognizing know and remember from the past

showers brief rain fall

sprouting beginning to grow

Grammar

Action and Linking Verbs

An **action verb** tells what something or someone does. A **linking verb** tells what someone or something is.

Action verbs: *run, plays, laughs*

Linking verbs: *am, is, are, was, were*

Activity

Circle the Verbs Cut out a page from an old magazine. Together, find and circle the action verbs. Then find and underline the linking verbs.

Practice Tested Spelling Words

Cause and Effect • Story Structure

- A **cause** tells why something happened.
- An **effect** is what happened.
- Words such as *because* and *so* are clues that can help you figure out a **cause** and its **effects**.

Directions Read the following passage.

Pedro's family lives on a farm. His father grows corn for the family to enjoy. There is one important job that Pedro gets to do. He looks out for corn earworm moths.

These moths lay eggs in the corn and cotton crops. Their larvae eat the plants, destroying them. To keep the moths away, Pedro's father hires pilots to spray their fields with chemicals so the moths do not destroy the crops.

Because bats eat moths, they help guard the crop too. Mexican free-tailed bats live in caves near the fields. They can eat a thousand tons of moths in one night! That means fewer moths for Pedro to watch for, and more corn for his family to enjoy.

Directions Complete the cause and effect graphic organizer.

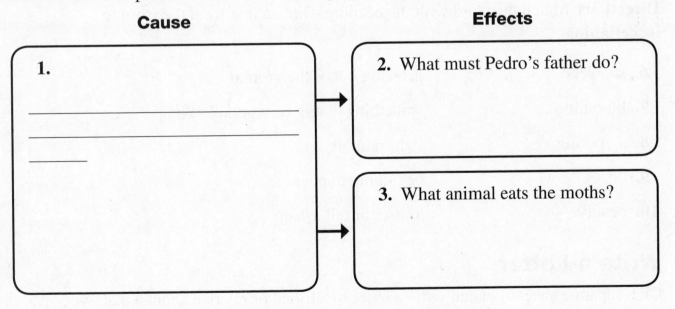

Cause

1.

_____

_____

Effects

2. What must Pedro's father do?

3. What animal eats the moths?

4. What pattern in the story helped you figure out the answers?

School + Home

Home Activity Your child found a cause and two effects in a passage. To help your child understand cause and effect, point out causes to your child and ask him or her to name the effects. For example, you might mention a rainy day as a cause. The effects could be using an umbrella and not being able to play outdoors.

© Pearson Education 3

Vocabulary

Check the Words You Know

___recognizing   ___humor
___doze   ___bulbs
___blooming   ___sprouting
___showers   ___beauty

Directions Fill in the blank with a word from the box that fits the meaning of the sentence.

1. You've grown so tall that I had trouble _____ you.

2. I was so tired that I began to _____ while sitting in a chair.

3. The _____ I planted last fall will come up as flowers in the spring.

4. Anyone who laughs at my jokes must have a good sense of _____ .

5. All the flowers were pretty, but the red one was a real _____ .

Directions Match the word with its meaning. Draw a line from the word to its definition.

6. showers   growing out of the ground

7. blooming   something that is very good looking

8. sprouting   light rainfall

9. doze   beginning to open

10. beauty   to nap, or fall asleep

Write a Letter

On a separate sheet of paper, write a letter to a friend or relative about a plant you would like to grow. Use as many vocabulary words as possible.

School + Home

Home Activity Your child identified and used vocabulary from *The Gardener*. Read a story about urban gardens to your child. Discuss the story, using this week's vocabulary words.

Vocabulary • Word Structure

- Sometimes you can figure out the meaning of unfamiliar words by looking at the **word structure**. Some words have an -s ending to show more than one. Some words have an -ed ending to show that something happened in the past.
- Use **word endings** to help you figure out the meaning of unfamiliar words.

Directions Read each sentence. Underline the noun with the -s ending that shows more than one.

1. I sent my grandmother a picture of a bunch of flowers.

2. I miss my grandmother, but I like writing letters to her.

3. There are three trees in my front yard.

4. I planted carrot seeds in my garden.

5. We planted one bulb in each of the pots.

Directions Read each sentence. Underline the verb with the -ed ending that shows what happened in the past.

6. Yesterday, I planted four rows of corn.

7. I pushed the seeds down carefully into the ground.

8. Then I covered the seeds with some soil.

9. After two weeks, the first tiny sprouts appeared.

10. All my corn plants survived, and now we eat fresh corn.

Home Activity Your child identified and used new words by understanding word structure and the endings -s and -ed. Read a story with your child. Encourage your child to identify unfamiliar words with these endings, and then help your child figure out the meaning of the words.

Draw Conclusions

- A **conclusion** is a decision you reach that makes sense after you think about details or facts in what you read.
- As you read, think about the details and make decisions about the characters and what happens in the story.

Directions Read the following letter. Then answer the questions below.

> Dear Cousin Howie,
> We traveled all summer. We finally arrived here at the end of August. Wildflowers were blooming everywhere. The prairie has a beauty of its own.
> Before snow fell, we planted bulbs. We had our prized tulips in the spring. You wouldn't believe the showers we had this spring. We plowed and planted the muddy fields anyway. I got so tired that I dozed off at supper every night.
> The grains are sprouting now. Can you come out to help us with the August harvest?
> Yours,
> Jonathan

1. Using what you know, what are Jonathan and his family doing?

_____

2. How do you know that cousins Jonathan and Howie are close friends?

_____

3. What fact tells you that before moving, Jonathan did not live on the prairie?

_____

4. Why was Jonathan so tired in the spring?

_____

5. How does the text structure help you know that the two cousins live far away?

_____

_____

Home Activity Your child had to draw conclusions to answer questions. A conclusion is a decision the reader reaches after thinking about the passage's details and facts. The reader also uses prior knowledge to draw conclusions. After reading together, ask questions that require your child to use facts and prior knowledge to come to a conclusion about the story's characters and events.

© Pearson Education 3

Cause and Effect • Story Structure

- A **cause** tells why something happened.
- An **effect** is what happened.
- Words such as *because* and *so* are clues that can help you figure out a **cause** and its **effects**.

Directions Read the following letter. Then answer the questions below.

Dear June,
    I've been helping Mom and Dad in the flower shop. We grow flowers and sell them to customers.
    Yesterday, our cat Boots got into the shop. She left dirty tracks everywhere because her feet were muddy from running through the gardens. We tried to catch her.

When I chased her, she jumped up on the shelves. She knocked down several vases, and they broke.
    So now we have to put Boots in the basement before we open the shop in the morning.

Love, Nellie

1. What happened when Boots got into the flower shop?

_____

2. What did Boots do when Nellie tried to catch her?

_____

3. Why did the vases break?

_____

4. Why does Boots have to go to the basement now?

_____

5. What pattern in the text helps you find cause and effect?

_____

Home Activity Your child answered questions about causes and effects in a story and found clue words that tell about cause-and-effect relationships. Ask your child to make up sentences using the words *because* and *so*. Then have your child identify the cause and effect in each pair of sentences.

© Pearson Education 3

Cause and Effect

- A **cause** tells why something happened.
- An **effect** is what happened.
- Words such as *because* and *so* are clues that can help you figure out a **cause** and its **effects**.

Directions Read the following passage.

"**Y**ou're going to go to camp this summer," said Mom. "You need to get out of the city."

So Shante went to a camp in the country. She went swimming in a lake. She hiked in the mountains and picked wildflowers.

The air was clean and crisp. When she got home, her mother said, "You look so healthy because you went to camp. You got lots of exercise and breathed clean air. You're not coughing from the city smoke."

Directions Complete the cause and effect graphic organizer.

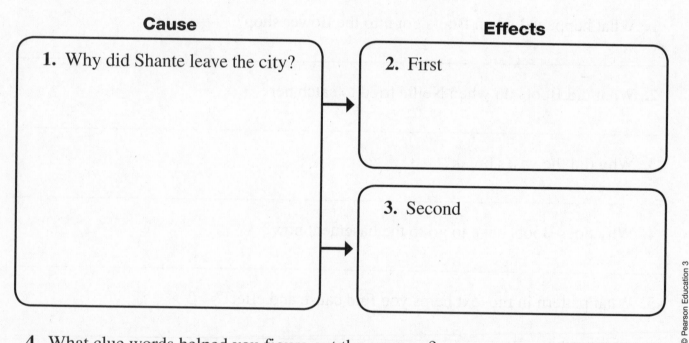

Cause

1. Why did Shante leave the city?

Effects

2. First

3. Second

4. What clue words helped you figure out the answers?

© Pearson Education 3

Contractions

Directions Use each pair of words to make a contraction. Write the contraction on the line.

_____ **1.** have not

_____ **2.** when is

_____ **3.** did not

_____ **4.** they will

_____ **5.** she is

_____ **6.** you will

_____ **7.** we would

_____ **8.** I would

_____ **9.** let us

_____ **10.** they are

_____ **11.** that is

_____ **12.** he would

_____ **13.** was not

_____ **14.** you would

Directions: Use the words in ( ) to make a contraction to complete each sentence. Write the contraction on the line.

_____ **15.** Judy (has not) planted a garden before.

_____ **16.** This year she decided (she would) like to grow some plants.

_____ **17.** Her mom said that (they would) work together.

_____ **18.** Judy's mom told her that it (was not) yet time to plant the garden.

_____ **19.** She explained that seeds can't grow if (it is) too cold.

_____ **20.** She also said that plants (would not) grow without water.

 Home Activity Your child formed contractions by using an apostrophe to take the place of letters that are left out. Ask your child to think of at least ten other word pairs that can be used to form contractions, such as *she is (she's), we will (we'll),* and *are not (aren't).* Ask your child to write sentences using these contractions.

Card Catalog and Library Database

Libraries use a **card catalog** or a computerized **library database** to organize their materials. You can search for a book using the **author, title,** or **subject.** Look for the author's last name followed by the first name. When the book is located, either on the card or computer, there will be a **call number.** Each book in the library has its own call number that appears on the spine of the book.

Directions A database entry for a book on gardening is shown below. Use the entry to answer the questions.

Main Menu	Exit	Keyword Search	Browse	Advanced Search	Help

PUBLIC LIBRARY CARD CATALOG/DATABASE

Records 1 of 1
Gardening for Kids / by Patricia Farley
New York: Nature Publishing, 2005
CALL NUMBER: 536.2
Click on any of the following to start a new search: **Author / Title / Subject**

1. What would you type to search the database by author to find this book?

   _____

2. What is the call number for this book?

   _____

3. What would you type to search the database by subject to find this book?

   _____

4. You want to find a book about gardening. Which word will you click on to begin your search?

   _____

5. In which year was this book published?

   _____

© Pearson Education 3

Family Times

Summary

Pushing Up the Sky

Long ago, the sky was very close to Earth. This might sound like a lot of fun, but it was in the way. The chiefs all got together and had a meeting to decide what to do. It was decided that if they pushed together with long poles, they might succeed in pushing the sky out of the way. Their efforts moved the sky to where it is today!

Activity

What If the World Was Like That? Imagine that the world was very different in one way, much as the sky was very different in the story *Pushing Up the Sky*. What problems would this cause? Make up a play about the problem and the way you and your family would solve it.

Comprehension Skill

Author's Purpose

The **author's purpose** is the reason an author writes something. An author may write to persuade, to inform, to entertain, or to express ideas and feelings.

Activity

Topic Spin Think of a list of writing topics and write them down. Then make a spinner using a paper plate, a pencil, and a paper clip. Divide the spinner into four sections and write *inform*, *entertain*, *express*, and *persuade*, respectively, in each section. Players take turns picking a topic, spinning the spinner, and then describing what they could write with that topic and purpose.

Lesson Vocabulary

Words to Know

Knowing the meanings of these words is important to reading *Pushing Up the Sky*. Practice using these words.

Vocabulary Words

antlers one of two bony growths on the head of a deer and certain other animals

imagined formed pictures in a person's mind of things or ideas that are elsewhere or not real

languages spoken or written words

narrator a person who tells the story

overhead over the head; placed high up; above

poked pushed with something pointed; jabbed

Grammar

Main and Helping Verbs

Main verbs show the action in the sentences. **Helping verbs** can show the time of the action. *Have, has, had, will, is, am, are, was,* and *were* can be helping verbs. A verb phrase uses a main verb and a helping verb together.

We <u>were running</u>.

They <u>are climbing</u>.

The dogs <u>have barked</u> before.

Activity

Using Verb Phrases Write main verbs and helping verbs, each on an index card. Divide the cards into main verb and helping verb piles. Mix each pile and place the cards facedown. Each player takes the two top cards and creates a verb phrase. Then the player uses the verb phrase in a sentence. If the helping verb and main verb do not make sense together, return the helping verb to the bottom of the pile and choose another helping verb card until a phrase can be made that makes sense.

Practice Tested Spelling Words

Author's Purpose • Summarize

- The **author's purpose** is the reason an author writes something.
- An author may try to persuade, to inform, to entertain, or to express ideas and feelings.
- Different parts of a piece of writing may have different purposes.
- **Summarizing** the main ideas and details as you read can help you figure out the **author's purpose**.

Directions Read the following passage.

Northwest Indians were expert basket makers. They used baskets to store food, make food, and serve food. The baskets were woven so tightly they held water.

The people used thin sticks of wood or reeds. They wove grass or threads made from roots between the sticks. They pulled the threads tightly together.

If you ever go to the Northwest, you can see these baskets. You can buy them in stores. You can also see pictures of them on the Internet.

Directions Complete the chart. Give the author's purpose for each part. Then explain the purpose.

	Purpose	Why do you think so?
Beginning	Inform: give information about the baskets.	1. _____ _____
Middle	2. _____ _____	3. _____ _____
End	4. _____ _____	5. _____ _____

Home Activity Your child described the author's purpose for a piece of writing. Authors may have more than one purpose. The purpose of nonfiction is often to inform. Read nonfiction articles together. Ask your child to explain why the author wrote it. Remember, the author may have had more than one purpose.

© Pearson Education 3

Vocabulary

Directions Write the vocabulary word from the box next to its meaning.

_____ **1.** jabbed with a finger or stick

_____ **2.** someone who tells a story

_____ **3.** bonelike growths on an animal's head, such as a deer

_____ **4.** the words and grammar people use to communicate

_____ **5.** formed a picture in your mind about something

Directions Fill in the word from the box that fits the meaning of the sentence.

6. The deer had huge, pointed _____ on its head.

7. We looked at the clouds _____ to see if it would rain.

8. The boy _____ that he would grow up to be a great ball player.

9. My brother _____ me in the arm to wake me up.

10. Rafael speaks two _____, English and Spanish.

Write a Poem

On a separate sheet of paper, write a poem about something wonderful you imagine. Use as many vocabulary words as possible.

© Pearson Education 3

Home Activity Your child has identified and used vocabulary words from *Pushing Up the Sky*. Play a game with your child in which you take turns imagining something, with each of you adding to what the other imagined. Use as many vocabulary words as you can.

Vocabulary • Glossary

- Sometimes you can use a **glossary** to find the meaning of a word. A glossary gives the meanings of important words in a book.
- A **glossary** lists words and their meanings in alphabetical order.

---

coy•o•te (kī ō′tē), *NOUN.* a doglike wild animal of North America.

dis•ap•pear (dis′ə pir′), *VERB.* to vanish; to no longer be seen.

fierce (firs), *ADJECTIVE.* wild, untamed.

fire•brand (fīr′brand′), *NOUN.* a burning torch.

i•mag•ine (i maj′ən), *VERB.* to picture in your mind.

mis•er•a•ble (miz′ ər ə bəl), *ADJECTIVE.* feeling terrible.

rus•tle (rus′ əl), *VERB.* a sound of things gently rubbing together.

shiv•er (shiv′ər), *VERB.* to shake with cold.

Directions Read the story. Find the definition of the underlined words in the glossary.

Ray was lost in the woods. It was night, and it was cold. Ray <u>imagined</u> what it would be like to be warm at home. He was cold and <u>miserable</u>. He started to <u>shiver</u>. He was hungry too. Then he heard the bushes <u>rustle</u>. He looked up and saw a <u>coyote</u>. The coyote looked <u>fierce</u>, but he spoke kindly. "I will make you a fire," the coyote said.

The coyote brought wood and made a fire. Ray and the coyote sat warming themselves by the fire. Then the coyote said, "I will take you home." The coyote took a <u>firebrand</u> and led Ray out of the woods. Soon they were near Ray's house. "Goodbye," the coyote said. "Thank you very much," Ray said. Then he watched the coyote <u>disappear</u>.

1. imagined _____

2. miserable _____

3. shiver _____

4. rustle _____

5. coyote _____

6. fierce _____

7. firebrand _____

8. disappear _____

School + Home **Home Activity** Your child used a glossary to find the meaning of words. Read a nonfiction book with your child and encourage using the glossary to find the meanings of unfamiliar words.

Cause and Effect

- A **cause** is why something happened.
- An **effect** is something that happens.

Directions Read the following passage. Then answer the questions below.

Narrator Moose and Weasel use language to talk to each other in the woods they share.

Scene I Moose Gets Antlers

Moose My antlers finally grew in. I love having huge antlers overhead.

Weasel They make you taller. I wish I had antlers too.

Scene II Weasel Gets Antlers Too

Weasel I imagined antlers, and now I have them. They are so heavy on my head.

Moose They are too big for you. I hope you don't poke anyone with them.

Weasel If I wish it, they will go away.

1. Why are Moose and Weasel talking together in the woods?

_____

2. What effect do the antlers have on Weasel?

_____

3. How did Weasel get antlers?

_____

4. What two problems do the antlers cause Weasel?

_____

5. Write a summary of the play. Use the words *because* and *so*. How do the details help you find cause and effect? _____

_____

_____

Home Activity Your child identified causes and effects in a play. A cause is what made something happen. An effect is what happened. Ask questions about causes: What causes a cake to bake in an oven? (heat) What causes plants to grow? (the right amounts of sun and rain) Ask questions about effects. What makes a car run? (fuel)

116 Comprehension

Practice Book Unit 3

© Pearson Education 3

Author's Purpose • Summarize

- The **author's purpose** is the reason an author writes something.
- An author may try to persuade, to inform, to entertain, or to express ideas and feelings.
- Different parts of a piece of writing may have different purposes.
- **Summarizing** the main ideas and details as you read can help you figure out the **author's purpose**.

Directions Read the following passage. Then answer the questions below.

> Air contains oxygen, and people need oxygen to breathe. Smoke from factories and car exhaust makes the air dirty. This is called air pollution.
>
> Air is important to people. We need clean air to be healthy. A clean sky is beautiful too, and we need beauty in our lives.
>
> Please do what you can to keep the air clean. Instead of riding in a car, ride your bicycle. Walk to school or take the trolley.

1. What facts does the first paragraph contain?

_____

2. What is the purpose of the first paragraph?

_____

3. Why does the author write the second paragraph?

_____

4. What is the purpose of the last paragraph?

_____

5. Write a summary of the last paragraph. How does it help you figure out the author's purpose?

_____

_____

Home Activity Your child answered questions about the author's purpose. Find a letter to the editor in the newspaper and read it to your child. Ask him or her to explain why the author wrote it. Discuss what your child might write about in a letter written to persuade.

© Pearson Education 3

Author's Purpose

- The **author's purpose** is the reason an author writes something.
- An author may try to persuade, to inform, to entertain, or to express ideas and feelings.
- Different parts of a piece of writing may have different purposes.

Directions Read the following passage.

> **Props** Use two blue blankets for the river. Put potted plants around the river as trees.
>
> **Narrator** People who lived near the river fished for salmon. Salmon was an important part of their diet.
>
> **Man** That fish looks tasty. I want to catch that fish.
>
> **Salmon** Use a net.
> (Man puts net in river. Salmon jumps over it.)
>
> **Salmon** I don't want to be caught today. I want to swim upstream instead.
>
> **Man** The joke is on me.

Directions Complete the chart. Give the author's purpose for each part. Then explain the purpose.

	Purpose	Why do you think so?
Beginning (Props)	**Inform: Tell how to make the props.**	1. The sentences after "Props" _____ _____
Middle (Narrator)	2. Inform: _____ _____	3. The narrator tells _____ _____ _____
End (Man and Salmon)	4. _____ _____	5. The play made me _____ _____

Home Activity Your child found the author's purpose for three different parts of a play. Read another play. Ask your child to explain the purpose of its different parts. Remember that an author may have more than one reason for writing a play. Some parts of a play inform the reader. Other parts are meant to entertain, persuade, or express feelings.

Prefixes un-, re-, mis-, dis-

Directions Add the prefix **un-, re-, mis-,** or **dis-** to each base word. Write the new word on the line.

1. un- + load = _____

2. re- + act = _____

3. mis- + direct = _____

4. un- + roll = _____

5. dis- + like = _____

Directions Write the word from the box that best fits each definition.

_____ **6.** to spell wrong

_____ **7.** not agree

_____ **8.** not known

_____ **9.** to write again

_____ **10.** not honest

> disagree
> dishonest
> misspell
> rewrite
> unknown

Directions Add the prefix **un-, re-, mis-,** or **dis-** to the word in ( ) to complete each sentence. Write the new word on the line.

_____ **11.** Last night I was (able) to see the stars.

_____ **12.** The sky was so dark, I thought they had (appeared).

_____ **13.** I couldn't use the telescope. Someone had (placed) it.

_____ **14.** When I asked who had used the telescope last, no one could (call).

_____ **15.** It's (likely) that I will see the stars tonight.

Home Activity Your child wrote words with the prefixes *un- (unhappy)*, *re- (recall)*, *mis- (mistake)*, and *dis- (dislike)*. Ask your child to choose words from the box above and use them in sentences. Then ask your child to remove the prefix from each word and use the new words in sentences.

Thesaurus

A **thesaurus** includes entry words with synonyms (words with the same or similar meanings) and antonyms (words with opposite meanings). Most word processing programs have a thesaurus to help you choose just the right word.

Directions Use the thesaurus entry to answer the questions.

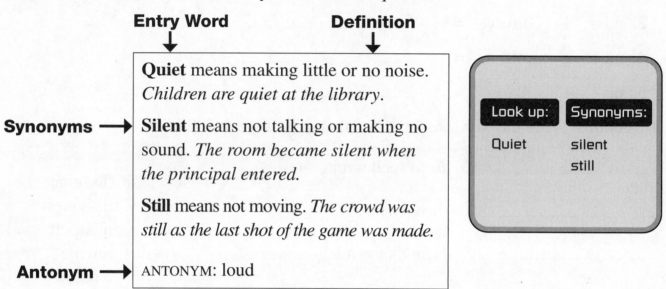

Entry Word   **Definition**

Quiet means making little or no noise. *Children are quiet at the library.*

Synonyms → **Silent** means not talking or making no sound. *The room became silent when the principal entered.*

Still means not moving. *The crowd was still as the last shot of the game was made.*

Antonym → ANTONYM: loud

Look up: Quiet   Synonyms: silent   still

1. What is the entry word for this thesaurus example?

_____

2. Which synonym of *quiet* best completes this sentence?
   Peter stood very _____ as the angry dog approached.

_____

3. Which word could you use to replace the underlined phrase in this sentence?
   The children on the playground were <u>not quiet</u>.

_____

4. How could you use a thesaurus to find more antonyms for *quiet*?

_____

5. What is one way that you could use a thesaurus for schoolwork?

_____

Home Activity Your child answered questions about a thesaurus entry. Read a book or story with your child. Select appropriate words for him or her to look up in a thesaurus to find synonyms and antonyms.

Family Times

Summary

Night Letters

Lily loves to look at the critters and plants she finds in nature. When she looks carefully at their fine details, she feels like they are talking to her in a secret code. She writes what she observes in her nature journal. Her last message of the day comes from a tree that asks her to return tomorrow. She replies with a promise of more visits the next day.

Activity

What Does Nature Tell You? This week, spend some time together in a quiet spot in nature. Draw what you see and jot down a few words about what you feel. Compare your drawings and ideas.

Comprehension Skill

Draw Conclusions

A **conclusion** is a decision you reach after thinking about **facts** and **details** you know. You can use what you have learned in the story and **what you already knew** before you began to read.

Activity

Nature Walk Take a nature walk together. Look for clues about the local wildlife. Is there evidence of raccoons? Are there more birds in one yard than another? Use what you know about and what you see around you to draw conclusions about these critters.

Lesson Vocabulary

Words to Know

Knowing the meanings of these words is important to reading *Night Letters*. Practice using these words.

Vocabulary Words

blade a leaf of grass

budding beginning to form a flower

dew moisture from the air that forms drops on cool surfaces

fireflies small beetles that fly at night and give off short flashes of light from their bodies

flutter to move or fly with quick, light, flapping movements

notepad a pad of paper with blank pages for notes

patch a small piece of ground where something grows

Grammar

Subject-Verb Agreement

The **subject** and **verb** in a sentence must work together, or **agree.** To make most present tense verbs agree with singular subjects, add -*s*. If the subject is a plural noun or pronoun, the present tense verb does not end in -*s*.

Activity

Let's Agree to Agree Write the subjects and verbs below on index cards. Keep the subjects and verbs in separate piles. Mix each pile and spread them facedown on a table. Players take turns flipping over one card from each pile and reading the words. If the subject and verb agree, the player keeps the pair. If the cards don't agree, then the cards are turned facedown and play goes to the next player.

Subjects		Verbs	
he	they	talk	talks
you (singular)	it	are	is
she	we	does	do
I	you (plural)	am	can

Practice Tested Spelling Words

_____ _____ _____ _____

_____ _____ _____ _____

_____ _____ _____ _____

_____ _____ _____ _____

_____ _____ _____ _____

Draw Conclusions • Ask Questions

- A **conclusion** is a decision you reach after thinking about facts and details you read.
- You can also use **what you already know** to help draw a conclusion.
- Then **ask yourself,** "Does my conclusion make sense?"

Directions Read the following passage. Complete the chart to draw a conclusion.

Plants need food, water, and sunlight to grow. Most plants make their food from the sun. Venus's-flytraps have a special way to get their food.

Venus's-flytraps trap and digest insects! Their leaves snap shut in an instant when something crawls inside. The insect's movements set off the plant's trigger hairs.

Venus's-flytrap leaves grow close to the ground. A tall stem grows from them. In the spring, white flowers bloom at the top of the stem. Insects, such as honeybees, help by carrying pollen from one Venus's-flytrap to the next.

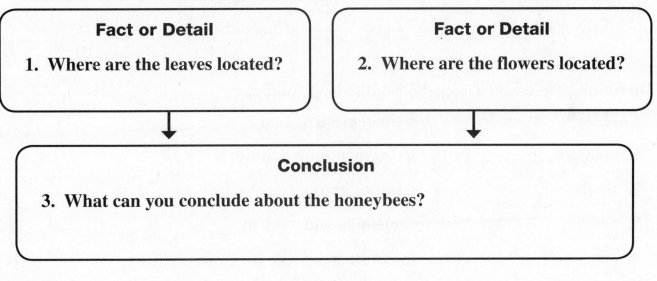

Fact or Detail

1. Where are the leaves located?

Fact or Detail

2. Where are the flowers located?

Conclusion

3. What can you conclude about the honeybees?

4. Does your conclusion make sense? Explain why.

_____

_____

5. Tell how asking questions helped you make a good conclusion.

_____

Home Activity Your child drew conclusions by using facts or details in a selection combined with what he or she already knows. Draw another graphic organizer like the one above. Write two facts or details in the top parts. For example, you might write "A plant is dry" and "It hasn't rained for a long time." Then help your child draw the conclusion that the plant needs water.

Name _____

Vocabulary

Check the Words You Know

_____ blade   _____ flutter
_____ fireflies   _____ patch
_____ dew   _____ budding
_____ notepad

Directions Read each question. Then fill in the bubble next to the correct answer.

1. What is a piece of grass?
   - ( ) a branch
   - ( ) a blade
   - ( ) a flower

2. What is a small piece of ground?
   - ( ) dew
   - ( ) flutter
   - ( ) patch

3. The word *flutter* means
   - ( ) to stop and wait
   - ( ) to become flat
   - ( ) to flap wings quickly

4. What are the water drops found on a flower in the morning?
   - ( ) buds
   - ( ) dew
   - ( ) patch

Directions Draw a line from the word to its definition.

5. blade   a small piece of land

6. notepad   to begin to form a flower

7. fireflies   a leaf of grass

8. budding   something you write in

9. patch   insects that produce their own light

Write a Friendly Letter

Write a letter to an insect or animal you have seen. Tell something about your life. Use as many vocabulary words and compound words as you can in your letter.

Home Activity Your child identified and used vocabulary words from *Night Letters*. Work with your child to write a letter from the point of view of your pet or of an animal you've seen in your neighborhood. The letter should describe something about the animal's life. Use as many vocabulary words and compound words as possible in your letter.

Vocabulary • Word Structure

- Sometimes you may see words that are made up of two small words.
- Use the two small words to figure out the meaning of the **compound word.**

Directions Read each sentence. A compound word is underlined in each. Circle the two small words that make up the underlined compound word.

1. I use a <u>notepad</u> to list things I need to buy.

2. I grow lots of flowers in my <u>backyard</u> garden.

3. On summer nights, I love to watch the blinking <u>fireflies</u>.

4. We picked <u>blackberries</u> that my mother will use to make jam.

5. I need to use a <u>flashlight</u> when I go down into the dark basement.

6. I carry my school books in my <u>backpack</u>.

7. The squirrel made a <u>treetop</u> nest near my window.

8. We decorated our <u>classroom</u> with pictures of animals.

Directions Think of five compound words. Write a sentence for each word. Circle each compound word in your sentences.

9. _____

_____

10. _____

_____

11. _____

_____

12. _____

_____

13. _____

_____

Home Activity Your child identified and used compound words. Read a story or nonfiction book about insects. Encourage your child to identify and define compound words in the story.

Author's Purpose

- The **author's purpose** is the reason an author writes something. Some reasons are to persuade, to inform, to entertain, or to express ideas and feelings.
- Different parts of a piece of writing may have **different purposes.**

Directions Read the following passage. Then answer the questions below.

In the morning, Tommy took his notepad with him as he walked to school. He saw some dew on a blade of grass. Tommy stopped to draw a picture of it. "Dew on a blade of grass," he wrote in his notepad.

After school, Tommy saw a luna moth. He drew a picture of it in his notepad. "Luna moths are pale green," he wrote. "Their hindwings have long curving tails."

That night, Tommy sat in the backyard. Fireflies swirled around him. Tommy drew a picture of a firefly in his notepad. "Fireflies flutter their wings to stay in the air," he wrote.

Tommy saw that the apple trees were budding. He drew the buds. After many days, his notepad was filled up. Then Tommy started another one.

1. What is the purpose of the first paragraph?

_____

2. Why do you think the author tells us what Tommy wrote in his notepad?

_____

3. What did you learn about luna moths in the second paragraph?

_____

4. Do you think the author most likely wrote this selection to teach or to inform? Explain your answer.

_____

_____

5. What question can you ask to find the author's purpose?

_____

Home Activity Your child answered questions about the author's purpose. Authors sometimes have more than one purpose for their writing. They may write to entertain, inform, express ideas and feelings, or persuade. While reading, stop to ask your child, "What is the author's purpose?" List the four reasons above if your child needs help.

© Pearson Education 3

Draw Conclusions • Ask Questions

- A **conclusion** is a decision you reach after thinking about facts and details you read.
- You can also use **what you already know** to help draw a conclusion.
- Then **ask yourself,** "Does my conclusion make sense?"

Directions Read the following passage. Then answer the questions below.

My friends and I started a nature writing club. We asked our parents to join us.

We hiked different trails every Saturday. We saw waterfalls, lakes, rivers, and streams. We saw trees, grasses, and wildflowers. We saw insects, birds, frogs, turtles, and small mammals. Sometimes Mike went fishing, but no one else did. While we were there, we wrote about what we saw. At the end of the year, we put all of our writing together to make a book.

1. Why do you suppose these friends wanted to start a nature writing club?

_____

_____

2. Why did they invite their parents to join them?

_____

_____

3. What do you think they wrote about?

_____

_____

4. Who most likely wrote about what it's like to go fishing? Explain.

_____

_____

5. Write a question about the book the club members made. Then draw a conclusion to answer your question.

_____

_____

_____

_____

Home Activity Your child answered questions that required drawing conclusions. Sometimes the answers to these questions are not found directly in the story. Your child must make a decision using details from the story along with prior knowledge.

Draw Conclusions

- A **conclusion** is a decision you reach after thinking about facts and details you read.
- You can also use what you already know to help draw a **conclusion.**
- Then ask yourself, "Does my **conclusion** make sense?"

Directions Read the following passage. Then complete the chart to draw a conclusion.

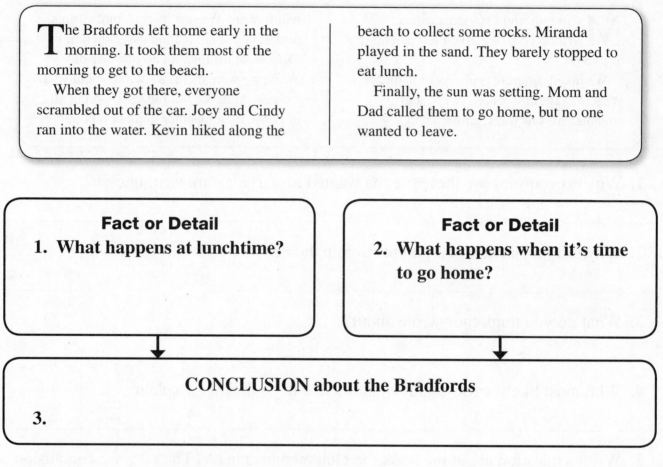

The Bradfords left home early in the morning. It took them most of the morning to get to the beach.

When they got there, everyone scrambled out of the car. Joey and Cindy ran into the water. Kevin hiked along the beach to collect some rocks. Miranda played in the sand. They barely stopped to eat lunch.

Finally, the sun was setting. Mom and Dad called them to go home, but no one wanted to leave.

Fact or Detail
1. What happens at lunchtime?

Fact or Detail
2. What happens when it's time to go home?

CONCLUSION about the Bradfords

3.

4. Does your conclusion make sense? Tell why.

_____

_____

Home Activity Your child drew a conclusion by using two facts or details from a story. Good readers draw conclusions as they read, using both facts in the story and their own prior knowledge. Provide your child with two facts or details, such as "Sam fills up a tub with water" and "the dog runs away." Ask your child to use the information to draw a conclusion. (The dog does not want to have a bath.)

Spellings of /j/, /k/, /s/

Directions Underline the letter or letters that stand for the sound /j/ in **jar**, **large**, and **edge**. Then write a sentence using each word.

1. damage

_____

2. bridge

_____

3. banjo

_____

4. village

_____

Directions Circle the words in the box that have the sound /k/ spelled *k*, *c*, *ck*, and *ch* as in **mar_k_**, **_c_ost**, **pi_ck_**, and **_sch_ool**. Write the words on the lines below.

> brake   branch   cellar   decide   locket
> merchant   peaceful   stomach   stretch   stuck

5. _____   **7.** _____

6. _____   **8.** _____

Directions Choose the words with the sound /s/ as in **per_s_on** and **pen_c_il**. Write the word on the line.

_____   **9.** acid   is   picture

_____   **10.** become   catch   inside

_____   **11.** coat   dance   was

_____   **12.** account   bacon   once

© Pearson Education 3

School + Home   **Home Activity** Your child wrote words with the /j/ sound in *jar*, *large*, and *edge*, the /s/ sound in *person* and *pencil*, and the /k/ sound in *mark*, *cost*, *pick*, and *chorus*. Encourage your child to identify other words with the /j/, /s/, or /k/ sounds. Together, make a list of these words and use them in sentences.

Adjust Reading Rate

When you read for different purposes, it helps to **adjust your reading rate.** If you are reading a science book with unfamiliar words, you may want to read slowly. Reading slowly also helps when studying for a test. Read quickly when you are skimming for important words or the main idea.

Directions Adjust your reading rate to answer the questions.

---

370 Part 5/Atmospheric Conditions

Clouds
As warm air rises and cools, clouds are formed at different levels above the ground. Clouds are grouped by their shape and height above the ground. There are high-, medium-, and low-level clouds.

High-Level Clouds usually form higher than 20,000 feet above sea level. They are formed mostly of ice crystals.

High-Level Clouds

cirrostratus

cirrus

cirrocumulus

---

1. How are clouds formed?

_____

2. How are clouds grouped?

_____

3. How many feet above sea level do high-level clouds appear?

_____

4. How would you determine what this selection is mostly about?

_____

_____

5. Part of a science test is to describe the shapes of high-level clouds. How would you study for this part of the test?

_____

Home Activity Your child has learned to adjust his or her reading rate to answer questions about a reading selection. Ask your child to give examples of times when he or she might want to read something slowly. Also ask for examples of when he or she can skim, scan, and read text quickly.

Family Times

Summary

A Symphony of Whales

In this story, a young girl is gifted with the ability to hear whale songs. One night, she dreams that her sled dogs lead her to whales—and the next day they do. But the whales are in trouble! It is too late in the year for them to be this close to shore. They are trapped by ice, and each day they are in greater danger of either starving or suffocating. The girl and her people call for help from a Russian icebreaker ship. They break the ice, and they feed the whales their own food. With the help of the ship and a symphony of music, they save the whales from certain death.

Activity

What Would You Do? What animals would inspire you to the kind of hard work and sacrifice the Inuit village showed in saving these whales? Draw a picture of your favorite animals together.

Comprehension Skill

Generalize

When you read ideas about several things, you may see how they are alike in some way. You can make a **general statement** about all of them together.

Activity

Attributes Brainstorm three different characteristics in people. These can be physical or part of a personality. Then think of all the people you know with those characteristics and compose a sentence that summarizes these characteristics in a generalization. Finally, talk about other ways that these people may be alike. Can you think of other generalizations to make about this group of people?

Lesson Vocabulary

Words to Know

Knowing the meanings of these words is important to reading *A Symphony of Whales*. Practice using these words.

Vocabulary Words

anxiously nervously or in a worried manner

bay a part of an ocean enclosed by the coastline

blizzards heavy snowstorms with very strong winds

channel a body of water joining two larger bodies of water

chipped broke off small pieces of something

melody a series of musical notes that make up a tune

supplies quantities of something needed

surrounded encircled; enclosed

symphony a long musical work written for an orchestra

Grammar

Present, Past, and Future Tense

Verbs can show action. They can also show when the action happens. Different verb tenses have different forms. Many **present tense verbs** end in -*s*. You form the **past tense** of most verbs by adding -*ed*. The **future tense** tells what will happen in the future. When you add the helping verb *will* to a verb, you make it a future tense verb. You also can use the future tense when you want to tell about what probably will happen.

Activity

The Present, Past, and Future Family Each player takes on the identity of one of the tenses. For example, you might have a Mr. Present, Mrs. Past, and Master Future. The player representing the present thinks of a verb and uses it in a sentence. Then the players representing past and future must each change the verb to their tense and use the word correctly in the same sentence—modifying the sentence as needed.

Practice Tested Spelling Words

_____   _____   _____   _____

_____   _____   _____   _____

_____   _____   _____   _____

_____   _____   _____   _____

_____   _____   _____   _____

Generalize • Answer Questions

- Ideas in what you read are sometimes alike in several ways. To **generalize**, you can make a general statement about them together.
- Look for **clue words** like *most*, *many*, *all*, *some*, or *few*.
- Ask and **answer questions** as you read to help you reach a **generalization**.

Directions Read the following passage.

Mammals are animals that need to breathe air. Most mammals give birth to live babies. Mammal mothers also give milk to their babies.

Gray whales live in the ocean. Mothers-to-be find a safe place, like a lagoon, to give birth. After the calf is born, a female helper pushes it up to the surface so it can breathe. Then the mother feeds the baby.

Directions Are gray whales mammals? Complete the chart. Make a generalization.

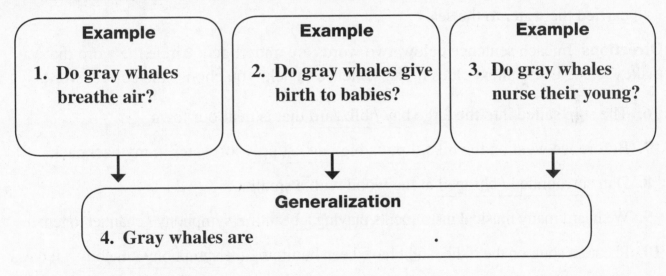

Example

1. Do gray whales breathe air?

Example

2. Do gray whales give birth to babies?

Example

3. Do gray whales nurse their young?

Generalization

4. Gray whales are _____ .

5. How did answering the questions in the examples help you make a generalization?

_____

© Pearson Education 3

Home Activity Your child made a generalization by finding examples of the ways things are alike. Draw a graphic organizer like the one above. Write examples about the ways dogs are alike in the three example boxes (dogs bark, wag tails, have hair). Then help your child write a generalization about dogs.

Name _____

Vocabulary

Directions Read the pairs of sentences below. Use one word from the box to fill in the blank in each pair of sentences. Use context clues to help you fill in the correct word.

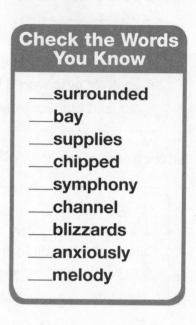

Check the Words You Know

___surrounded
___bay
___supplies
___chipped
___symphony
___channel
___blizzards
___anxiously
___melody

1. This winter was very snowy. We had four _____ in December alone!

2. The bird sang a beautiful tune. The _____ was sweet and sad.

3. The children gathered all around the teacher. She was _____ by her class.

4. She was worried about her grade on the test. She waited _____ as the tests were handed back.

5. The water flowed along a narrow stream. The stream was a _____ that carried the water to the sea.

Directions In each sentence below, two words are underlined. Circle the word that makes sense. Use context clues in the sentence to help you choose the correct word.

6. The ship sailed into the large bay / blizzard that is near our town.

7. Before we went on the hike, I put a big bay / supply of water in my backpack.

8. Dan surrounded / chipped at the wood with a small ax.

9. We heard many musical instruments playing a beautiful symphony / channel together.

10. I heard a song on the radio, and I have been humming the symphony / melody all day.

Write a Scene from a Play

On a separate sheet of paper, write a short scene from a play about a person communicating with an animal. Use as many vocabulary words as possible.

Home Activity Your child identified and used vocabulary words from *A Symphony of Whales*. Read a story or article about animals to your child. Have your child point out unfamiliar words. Work together to try to figure out the meaning of each word by using other words that appear near it.

Name _____

Vocabulary • Context Clues

- Sometimes when you are reading, you may come across a word you don't know.
- Look for **context clues** to find the meaning. Look at the words and sentences around the word for clues that tell you what the word means.

> anxiously bay blizzards channel chipped
> melody supplies surrounded symphony

Directions Match the word with its meaning. Draw a line from each word to its definition.

1. symphony   narrow stream of water

2. blizzards   music composed for an orchestra

3. channel   uneasily

4. melody   snowstorms

5. anxiously   tune

Directions Use a vocabulary word from the box to complete each sentence below. Write the word in the space.

6. We were _____ by the goats at the children's zoo.

7. Thomas had _____ away the ice with the shovel.

8. Zak sailed his boat into the _____ safe from the ocean's waves.

9. The campers had enough _____ for three days.

10. Grandpa whistled a catchy _____.

Home Activity Your child identified and used context clues to understand new words in text. Read a story or article about animals to your child. Have your child point out unfamiliar words. Work together to try to figure out the meaning of each word by using other words that appear near it.

Draw Conclusions

A **conclusion** is a decision you reach that makes sense after you think about details or facts and what you already know.

Directions Read the following passage. Then answer the questions below.

Sandy heard about the whales, so she hurried down to the bay. Instead of swimming out to sea, whales had gone through the channel. Now the whales were marooned.

When she got there, people already surrounded the whales. Sandy helped chip ice to free them.

Firefighters brought hoses and other supplies. The tide was rising. Everyone waited anxiously to see what would happen.

The swish of water from the hoses sounded like a symphony. The water melted the ice. The whales wiggled loose. They swam out to sea. Everyone cheered.

1. Why did Sandy hurry to the bay?

_____

2. What does *marooned* mean?

_____

3. How did the whales get in trouble?

_____

4. Why were firefighters called to rescue the whales?

_____

5. What detail tells you that the people were happy that the whales were freed?

_____

_____

© Pearson Education 3

Home Activity Your child answered questions about a story that required drawing conclusions. Drawing conclusions means reaching a decision using facts and details in the story. A conclusion should also make sense. Give your child a faulty conclusion, such as "The best day to go to the beach is a rainy day." Ask your child to correct the sentence and give a reason. "The best day is a sunny day because people go to the beach to enjoy the sun."

Generalize

- Ideas in what you read are sometimes alike in several ways. To **generalize,** you can make a general statement about them together.
- Look for **clue words** like *most, many, all, some,* or *few.*
- Ask and **answer questions** as you read to help you reach a **generalization.**

Directions Read the following passage. Then answer the questions below.

Tameika wrote a report on gray whales. She said that gray whales do not have teeth. They feed by filtering shellfish from the ocean bottom through thin plates in their mouths.

Byron wrote a report on killer whales. He said that killer whales have teeth. They hunt other sea animals.

The two students exchanged reports. "How can killer whales hunt when gray whales do not?" Byron asked Tameika.

Tameika and Byron looked in an encyclopedia. Here's what they found: *Some whales hunt for food. Others strain small prey from ocean waters through plates in their mouths.*

1. What example of eating was in Tameika's report?

_____

_____

2. What example of eating was in Byron's report?

_____

3. What part of the story is a generalization about the way whales eat?

_____

4. What clue word tells you that a generalization is being made?

_____

5. How did the question Byron asked help the two students generalize?

_____

Home Activity Your child answered questions about the process of making generalizations. To make a generalization, you must read a passage with several examples. Find a book or magazine article that tells about different kinds of birds (or flowers). After reading, make a generalization about them.

Generalize

- Ideas in the things you read are sometimes alike in several ways. To **generalize,** you make a general statement about them.
- Look for **clue words** like *most, many, all,* or *few.*

Directions Read the following passage.

Mrs. Jones took her class to a sea animal park. "Animals that breathe through a blowhole are whales," she said. "Find the animals that are whales."

The students watched the show. Porpoises came up for food. They all blew air out of blowholes.

Next, a man swam with dolphins. Before the dolphin went underwater, it took a breath. Then it closed its blowhole.

Then orcas raced around the pool. One orca jumped out of the water. The students saw its blowhole when it fell back into the water.

"Now we know some sea animals that are whales," the students said.

Directions Complete the chart to make a generalization.

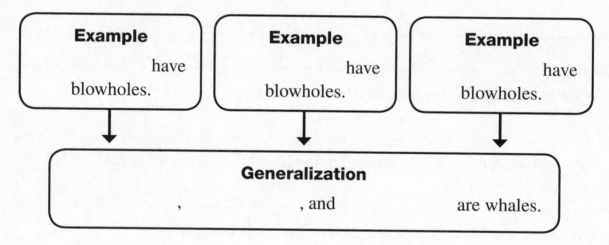

Example
_____ have blowholes.

Example
_____ have blowholes.

Example
_____ have blowholes.

Generalization
_____ , _____ , and _____ are whales.

Home Activity Your child made a generalization by looking for examples in a story. To make a generalization, a reader must look at several ideas and find a way that they are alike. Tell your child that animals with feathers are birds. Look for birds as you take a walk. Have your child make a generalization about them.

© Pearson Education 3

Suffixes -ly, -ful, -ness, -less

Directions Add the suffix **-ly, -ful, -ness,** or **-less** to each base word. Write the new word on the line.

1. grace   +   -ful   =   _____

2. bare   +   -ly   =   _____

3. worth   +   -less   =   _____

4. fair   +   -ness   =   _____

5. play   +   -ful   =   _____

6. wire   +   -less   =   _____

7. rare   +   -ly   =   _____

8. neat   +   -ness   =   _____

Directions Add **-ly, -ful, -ness,** or **-less** to the base word in ( ) to best complete each sentence. Use the word box for help. Write the new word on the line.

> careful   careless   illness   quickly   safely   spotless   thickness

_____ **9.** A (care) mistake can cause an oil spill at sea.

_____ **10.** This can (quick) cause problems for seabirds.

_____ **11.** In order to fly, birds need to keep themselves (spot).

_____ **12.** If the oil is not (safe) removed, the birds cannot fly.

_____ **13.** If a seabird swallows oil, it can develop an (ill).

_____ **14.** The (thick) of a bird's eggshell can also change.

_____ **15.** To protect the sea and its wildlife, ships' captains must be (care).

Home Activity Your child wrote words with the suffixes -ly (safely), -ful (playful), -ness (illness), and -less (worthless). Name some base words such as slow, thank, harm, kind, and help. Ask your child to make new words using the suffixes he or she practiced on this page.

Outlining and Summarizing

Summarizing is finding the most important ideas about a topic or text. You can summarize what you read or what you learn in class. One way to summarize is by making an **outline.** An outline shows a main idea and details, as in the one shown below.

An Endangered Animal—The African Elephant

I. Size
  A. Weight
    1. 7,000 to 15,000 pounds
    2. Males larger
  B. Height and Length
    1. 10 to 13 ft high
    2. 20 to 24 ft long

II. Diet—Vegetation
  A. Grasses
  B. Leaves
  C. Fruit

III. Habitat—Africa
  A. Forest
  B. Grassland

Directions Write the words from the box in the outline. Use the outline above as a guide.

Habitat	Deer	45 to 80 pounds	Rabbits	Wetlands

The Red Wolf

I. Size
  A. 4 1/2 to 5 1/2 ft long
  B. Weight
    1. _____
    2. Males larger

II. _____
  A. Forests
  B. Mountains
  C. _____

III. Diet
  A. Mainly small animals
    1. Rodents
    2. _____
  B. Others
    1. Insects
    2. Berries
    3. _____

© Pearson Education 3

Home Activity Your child learned how to make an outline to summarize ideas. Give your child information about a familiar topic. Include at least three main ideas and several details about the main ideas. Help him or her organize these ideas in an outline.

Family Times

Summary

Volcanoes

An active volcano destroys everything in its path. It can be a deadly force of nature even though it may look magnificent from a distance. Volcanoes occur because of the way that the surface of Earth moves over the melted rock below. The same forces cause earthquakes. Volcanoes happen where pressure builds so great that some of the melted rock comes to the surface. We still don't know how to predict when they will blow, but we know they will!

Activity

A Volcano's Good Side Hawaii has many active volcanoes. These volcanoes are sometimes destructive, but they are also the reason that Hawaii has numerous plants and animals. Together, research the connection between volcanoes and rich, fertile soil.

Comprehension Skill

Compare and Contrast

When you **compare** and **contrast** two or more things, you look for the ways they are alike and different.

Activity

Alike and Different Gather a variety of small household objects and place them in a box. Players take turns pulling two objects and naming ways the objects are alike and ways they are different. Return the objects to the box when you are done.

Lesson Vocabulary

Words to Know

Knowing the meanings of these words is important to reading *Volcanoes*. Practice using these words.

Vocabulary words

beneath under

buried covered up underground

chimney a natural or human-made hollow, vertical structure for the passage of smoke, gas, or fire

earthquakes sudden movements of Earth's crust followed by a series of shocks

fireworks explosions set off to create bright lights and colorful displays for entertainment

force power or energy

trembles vibrates; shakes

volcanoes openings in Earth's crust from which molten rock, dust, ash, and hot gases flow or erupt

Grammar

Irregular Verbs

Usually you add *-ed* to a verb to show action in the past. **Irregular verbs** do not follow this rule. Instead of ending in *-ed* to show past time, these verbs change to other words. When *have*, *has*, or *had* comes before these verbs, a third form of the word is used.

I *go*.
They *went*.
He has *gone*.

Activity

1, 2, 3 Whoops! Players take turns using the following words in sentences—incorrectly. The first player to correctly shout out the sentence using the correct form of the verb gets to think of the next mixed-up sentence.

present	past	past with have, has, had
write	wrote	written
speak	spoke	spoken
ring	rang	rung
see	saw	seen
take	took	taken

Practice Tested Spelling Words

_____ _____ _____ _____

_____ _____ _____ _____

_____ _____ _____ _____

_____ _____ _____ _____

_____ _____ _____ _____

Compare and Contrast • Monitor and Fix Up

- When you **compare** and **contrast**, you tell how two or more things are alike and how they are different.
- You can use a Venn diagram to **compare** and **contrast**.
- Reading slowly helps you notice details, key words, or other clues the author uses in **comparing** and **contrasting**.

Directions Read the following passage.

Have you ever been to Hawaii? If you go, you must see the volcanoes. There are many. Some are active. Others are not.

Mauna Loa is active. It covers half of an island. It is Earth's largest volcano. It last erupted, or blew up, in 1984.

Kilauea is Earth's most active volcano. It erupted in 1983 and it is still erupting. The fires are still burning. It is the longest-lived volcano. It is also the youngest one on the island.

Directions Complete the Venn diagram to compare and contrast. Use these words:
volcanoes, youngest, largest, longest-lived, most active

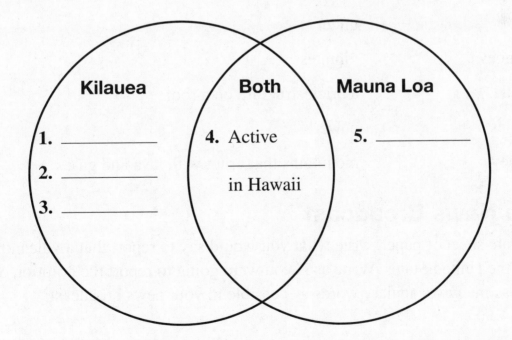

Kilauea
1. _____
2. _____
3. _____

Both
4. Active
_____
in Hawaii

Mauna Loa
5. _____

Home Activity Your child used a Venn diagram to compare and contrast volcanoes in Hawaii. Draw a Venn diagram together. Write "Active" in the first circle, "Inactive" in the second circle, and "Volcanoes" where the two circles overlap. Ask your child to explain the differences between an active and inactive volcano using the diagram.

Vocabulary

Check the Words You Know

___beneath   ___earthquakes
___volcanoes   ___fireworks
___force   ___trembles
___chimney   ___buried

Directions Write the word from the box that matches the definition.

_____ **1.** shakes

_____ **2.** movements between two of Earth's plates

_____ **3.** a vent that lets out steam or smoke

_____ **4.** a display of burning, bright lights

_____ **5.** covered under earth or other material

Directions Draw a line from the word to its definition.

6. force   under

7. volcanoes   vibrates

8. beneath   a brick structure on a roof

9. trembles   power

10. chimney   mountains that erupt with lava and gases

Write a News Broadcast

On a separate sheet of paper, write what you would say to report that a volcano has erupted in the United States. Write as if you were going to report the eruption on TV news. Use as many vocabulary words as possible in your news broadcast.

Home Activity Your child identified and used vocabulary words from *Volcanoes*. Read a news report to your child that describes a natural event, such as a volcano, earthquake, storm, or flood, that occurred somewhere in the world. Talk about the event using this week's vocabulary words.

© Pearson Education 3

Vocabulary • Dictionary

- You can use a **dictionary** to find the meaning of unfamiliar words.
- The words in a **dictionary** are listed in **alphabetical order**.

Directions Read the sentences below. One word is underlined. Use the sample dictionary page to write the definition of the underlined word on the line.

> **earthquake • volcano**
> **earthquake** *n.* a movement of the plates that make up Earth's crust
> **erupt** *v.* to explode outward
> **lava** *n.* melted rock that flows from a volcano
> **predict** *v.* to make a statement about what will happen later
> **trembles** *v.* shakes
> **volcano** *n.* a mountain that erupts, shooting lava, rocks, and hot ash onto Earth's surface

1. Scientists knew that the volcano was about to <u>erupt</u>.

_____

2. The <u>volcano</u> shot hot ash high into the air.

_____

_____

3. Scientists can <u>predict</u> when an earthquake will occur.

_____

4. The <u>earthquake</u> damaged a lot of buildings in the city.

_____

5. During an earthquake, the surface of the earth above it <u>trembles</u>.

_____

6. Some volcanoes send streams of <u>lava</u> flowing over the ground.

_____

Home Activity Your child identified and used vocabulary words from *Volcanoes*. Read a story or nonfiction book about earthquakes or volcanoes. Encourage your child to use a dictionary to find the meaning of unfamiliar words.

Author's Purpose

- The **author's purpose** is the reason an author writes something.
- An author may try to persuade, inform, entertain, or express feelings.

Directions Read the following passage. Then answer the questions below.

Mount Vesuvius is a volcano in Italy. It is an old, active volcano.

The volcano was quiet for a long time. People living nearby did not think it was active. But it erupted with great force in A.D. 79. Fireworks of lava and ash escaped. Two cities were buried. Today you can see pictures of some of the things left behind. They tell how the people lived a long time ago.

The volcano erupted again 1,500 years later. With no warning, more people were killed.

Finally, scientists started to study the volcano. A lab was built to take measurements. When the volcano trembles, scientists know it is about to erupt. They are able to warn people.

When people nearby hear a warning, they leave the area and don't get hurt.

1. What is the purpose of the first paragraph?

_____

2. What is the purpose of the second paragraph?

_____

3. How does the third paragraph tell that the volcano is still dangerous?

_____

4. What is the purpose of the last paragraph?

_____

_____

5. Scientists today can warn people when a volcano is about to erupt. In which part of the passage did you learn that?

_____

School + Home **Home Activity** Your child answered questions to help understand the author's purpose. Read a story or article with your child and have him or her identify author's purpose.

Compare and Contrast • Monitor and Fix Up

- When you **compare** and **contrast,** you tell how two or more things are alike and different.
- Reading slowly helps you notice details, key words, and clues used to **compare** and **contrast**.

Directions Read the following passage. Then answer the questions below.

> We used to live in Florida where hurricanes brought wind, rain, and flooding. A television announcer told us when one was coming. We taped boards over our windows so they wouldn't break. Sometimes we got into our car and went to a safer place. Other times we stayed inside until the bad weather was over.
>
> Now we live in California. We have earthquakes here. The ground shakes. The walls and windows rattle in our apartment. Sometimes papers and even spoons and cups fall off the table! In a bad earthquake, our building could fall down. We run outside to keep safe. But usually the earthquake is just a small tremor.

1. Write the topic for each paragraph.

_____

2. How are California and Florida different?

_____

3. How are earthquakes and hurricanes different?

_____

_____

4. In what ways are hurricanes and earthquakes alike?

_____

5. For which dangerous event do people usually get a warning?

_____

Home Activity Your child answered questions that required comparing and contrasting. Have your child pick two items, perhaps two games. Talk about how the games are alike and different. Use the words *compare* and *contrast*.

© Pearson Education 3

Name _____

Compare and Contrast

- When you **compare** and **contrast**, you tell how two or more things are alike and how they are different.
- You can use a Venn diagram to **compare** and **contrast**.

Directions Read the following passage.

Have you ever gone sledding? Then you know that things can slide down steep slopes. Earth, rocks, gravel, mud, and snow can slide down steep slopes, too.

A mud slide happens after lots of rain. A slope gets muddy, and the mud starts to slide downhill. So much mud can slide downhill that houses at the bottom can get covered in mud!

Slides happen in snowy mountains, too. First, a blizzard drops a lot of snow. The heavy snow starts to slide. When lots of snow slides all together, it is called an avalanche.

Directions Complete the Venn diagram to compare and contrast. Use these words: *snow, rain, blizzard, mud*. Write in the center what both have in common.

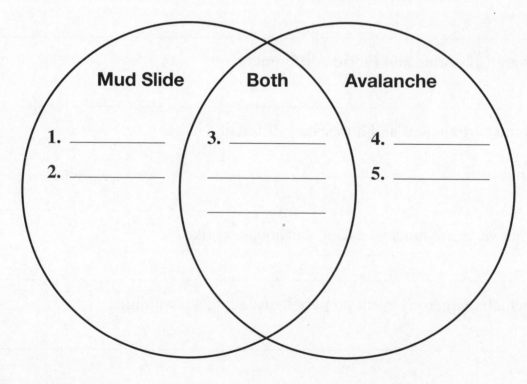

Mud Slide

1. _____
2. _____

Both

3. _____

_____

Avalanche

4. _____
5. _____

Home Activity Your child used a Venn diagram to compare and contrast two things. Draw a Venn diagram together. Write "Dogs" in the first circle, "Cats" in the second circle, and "Pets" where the two circles overlap. Ask your child to explain the differences between dogs and cats using the diagram.

Name _____

Silent Consonants

Directions Choose the word in ( ) with the silent consonant, as in **wr, kn, st, mb,** or **gn,** to complete each sentence. Write the word on the line.

_____ 1. It seemed like the perfect winter day for a (climb/hike) up the mountain.

_____ 2. Jan packed water and snacks in a (cooler/knapsack).

_____ 3. She put on her coat and (knit/new) cap.

_____ 4. She grabbed the scarf with the blue and yellow (design/stripes).

_____ 5. Then she (tossed/wrapped) it around her neck.

_____ 6. Jan began to (close/fasten) her coat.

_____ 7. The radio was on, and Jan stopped to (hear/listen).

_____ 8. The reporter said there were (calls/signs) that a big snowstorm was on its way.

_____ 9. Jan (learned/knew) she would have to go hiking another day.

Directions Circle each word in the box that has a silent consonant. Write the circled words in alphabetical order on the lines below.

> gnaw relax castle wrong basket no comb knot humid water trap numb

10. _____   13. _____

11. _____   14. _____

12. _____   15. _____

Home Activity *Your child wrote words with the silent consonants wr (write), kn (knight), st (listen), mb (thumb), and gn (gnaw). Work with your child to see how many words with those silent letters you can name together. Write the words, and take turns making sentences using each word.*

Newsletter

Directions Read the newsletter. Use it to answer the questions below.

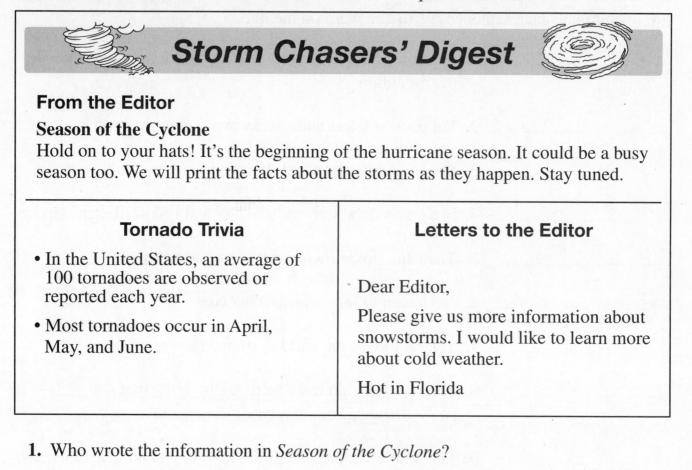

Storm Chasers' Digest

From the Editor

Season of the Cyclone
Hold on to your hats! It's the beginning of the hurricane season. It could be a busy season too. We will print the facts about the storms as they happen. Stay tuned.

Tornado Trivia

- In the United States, an average of 100 tornadoes are observed or reported each year.
- Most tornadoes occur in April, May, and June.

Letters to the Editor

Dear Editor,

Please give us more information about snowstorms. I would like to learn more about cold weather.

Hot in Florida

1. Who wrote the information in *Season of the Cyclone*?

_____

2. What is the name of the newsletter?

_____

3. What is included in the Tornado Trivia section?

_____

4. Why might someone write a letter to the editor?

_____

5. What other information might be included in this newsletter?

_____

Home Activity Your child read a newsletter and answered questions about it. Ask him or her to name some of the parts in a newsletter. Then have your child imagine that your neighborhood has its own newsletter. Encourage him or her to write a neighborhood news item.

Test-Taking Tips

1. Write your name on the test.

2. Read the directions carefully. Make sure you know exactly what you are supposed to do.

3. Read the question twice. Make sure you understand what the question is asking.

4. Read the answer choices for the question. Eliminate choices that do not make sense.

5. Mark your answer carefully.

6. Check your answer. Make sure that it makes the most sense out of all the answer choices.

7. If you have difficulty answering a question, you may want to go on to the next question. You can come back to difficult questions later.

8. If you finish the test early, go back and check all of your answers.

Name _____

Date	What is the title?	Who is the author?	What did you think of it?

© Pearson Education 3

Name _____

Reading Log

Date	What is the title?	Who is the author?	What did you think of it?

Name _____

Date	What is the title?	Who is the author?	What did you think of it?

Practice Book

Name _____

Date	What is the title?	Who is the author?	What did you think of it?

© Pearson Education 3

Name _____

Date	What is the title?	Who is the author?	What did you think of it?

Practice Book